Dopamine Detox

A Step-by-Step Guide to Overcome
Addictions, Break Bad Habits, and
Stop Obsessive Thoughts

Linda Hill

Linda Hill

Linda Hill

Table of Contents

Linda Hill

Your Secret Gift #1

Get My Next Book

"Dopamine Detox - Part 2"

(Free for a limited time)

For a limited time, and as a "Thank you" for purchasing this book, you can be added to our "Book 2 Launch List" for free so you get the second book of this series when it gets published (This book will be priced at $24.99 and I guarantee it will be a great read). Simply visit the URL below and follow the instructions. You'll be the first to get it.

Visit here:

lindahillbooks.com/detox

Scan QR Code:

Your Secret Gift #2

Get the Audio Version for Free

If you would like to get the audio version of this book so you can read along or listen while you are in the car, walking around, or doing other things, you're in luck. For a limited time, I've provided a link that will allow you to download this audiobook for FREE. (This offer may be removed at any time).

Step 1: Go to the URL below.

Step 2: Sign up for the 30-day free-trial membership (You may cancel at any time after, no strings attached)

Step 3: Listen to the audiobook

Visit here:

lindahillbooks.com/detoxpromo

Scan QR Code:

Introduction

Are you someone who feels constantly busy but never gets enough done? Do you find yourself gearing up to complete a task but before you know it, you are drowning in emails, to-do lists, or getting lost in your phone? Perhaps you find it hard to motivate yourself to achieve the goals that you truly desire. Instead of focusing on working toward your goals and ambitions, you get distracted from them and instead, lose yourself in the daily humdrum of life. Perhaps you find it difficult to concentrate and have picked up procrastination habits that are preventing you from getting what you really want out of life.

Well, there's a reason for that. Many of the activities we engage in day-to-day are not only hindering our progress, but are also having negative effects on our brain's dopamine levels. In fact, few people consider the negative impacts our tech-centered lives can have on our emotional well-being. Now in the 21st Century, smartphones have given us the ability to complete many of our daily tasks from one hand-held device. On the same half-hour bus ride, you can book a flight, read an excerpt from your favorite novel, check the stock market, and take a Zoom call, all from the comfort of your mobile phone.

So what's the problem?

While technology has undoubtedly improved many aspects of our lives, many modern daily habits are having a terrible impact on our brains. Many of our performative habits ensure that we are never fully focusing on the task at hand. Consider your daily habits and how you usually react to a single moment of downtime. It is not uncommon to be walking down the street while shooting off an email. Socializing with friends often includes posting the occasion on social media before the meet-up is even finished. Work days often include side-tracked time spent on researching your next holiday destination or reading celebrity gossip. The problem with these modern daily habits lies not in the habits themselves, but how these overstimulating activities make you *feel*.

The more we seek reward-based stimulation, the greater the desire for stimulation becomes. In other words, the modern world has people seeking more dopamine hits than ever before. This leaves our brains in constant overstimulation mode. If you are suffering from burnout, finding it hard to get motivated, and want to know how you can start getting your focus back, then this book is for you.

In Dopamine Detox, we will be learning what exactly dopamine is and what it does to the brain, as well as finding out which daily activities can overstimulate our dopamine production. This book will also focus on understanding how obsessive and negative thoughts can further instill procrastination habits that ultimately stop you from getting what you want out of life. We are going to investigate all types of addiction—from thoughts to smartphones to substances—and what happens to our dopamine levels when we are addicted to something. Then, I will teach you exactly what a dopamine detox is—step-by-step actionable methods to reduce your dopamine overstimulation and tried and tested methods that will help you avoid relapse. The methods written in this book have had clinical and measured success for many people. In fact, the very method of a "dopamine detox" has its scientific origins deriving from modern addiction services.

With the pandemic blurring the lines between work and home life—now more than ever—people are finding it hard to shut off. A huge number of workers have had to restructure their lives and create offices in spaces that also include household responsibilities such as chores, animals, and children. The societal expectation to constantly be available means that we are regularly engaging with dopamine overstimulation and this overindulgence is leaving us feeling miserable.

As we will learn in this book, dopamine is responsible for motivating our actions in return for a reward. Dopamine can be released by working on a project, interacting with loved ones, or creating something with our own artistic abilities. But technology has designed apps, television series, and games that give us a similar dopamine hit from less emotionally fulfilling tasks. The desire for pleasure is never satiated, and people are left wanting more and more.

This book will teach proven methods that will help you change your thinking patterns and challenge the addictions that are holding you back. We will investigate exactly how your dopamine levels are affected by your indulgences, learn how to recognize when you need a dopamine reset, practice some methodologies that will strengthen your concentration and productivity, and gain advice that will help you on your way to living a more balanced, productive lifestyle.

Are you ready to challenge the bad habits and negative thoughts that are holding you back? Then let's get started.

CHAPTER ONE

The Science of Dopamine

What is Dopamine?

Before we go any further, let's define what dopamine is and what our brain uses it for. Dopamine is a very important neurotransmitter that is connected to our brain's reward system. Dopamine creates a "call to action" that sends a message to our brain receptors to allow feelings of pleasure and satisfaction. However, it is not actually a pleasure chemical, despite some mistaking it as such. Dopamine release is not necessarily connected to our pleasure preference either. Rather, it allows for that pleasure or satisfaction to be felt in the first place. In other words, dopamine is the signal to our brain that pleasure is on its way. Hence, dopamine is the motivation for us to perform something, with the idea that pleasure will be the reward.

The brain has five main neural networks and dopamine interacts with many of them, including what's known as the **mesolimbic reward pathway**. Our brain networks need dopamine in order to perform properly. In the mesolimbic reward pathway, dopamine engages with our feelings and motivators around rewards, as well as movement, memory, motivation, and what we expect to happen. Dopamine also affects how prepared we are to be rewarded for meeting our goals.

Dopamine is essential for everyday activities. It influences our movement, the type of food and beverages we consume, how we take in information, and our likelihood of experiencing addiction issues. If you have ever wondered how we can teach animals—from rodents to cats and dogs—how to perform new tricks, it has a lot to do with dopamine. When the brain associates a given task with a reward, dopamine is released and it can give us the motivation to complete the task. If the brain does not think that a task is worth the reward, or if the reward feels too far away, then less dopamine is produced and the motivation to complete the task may be more difficult to find. When dopamine is produced, it helps channel our concentration, enhance our attention span, and keep our bodies moving. In fact, scientists believe that dopamine is the very reason we have not been wiped out as a species. Since it is connected to our means for survival and reproduction, dopamine is one of the main motivators in keeping us alive.

Dopamine is created in two parts of the brain. When it is produced, it sends a message to our brain receptors that associates an action with satisfaction or pleasure. This then trains the brain to perform this action over and over. It is the reason why animals can be taught to perform tricks by association and memory. Dopamine release will change behaviors—either of an animal or a human being—and will influence our motivation so that we can feel the satisfaction or pleasure that follows a task.

In this same sense, overstimulation of dopamine can lead to addiction to anything that causes its release. This could be an addiction to food, work, sex, drugs, and alcohol. The relation of dopamine to pleasure doesn't cause this so much as our *memory* of the pleasure felt when we engage with a certain external object. Since this neurotransmitter is associated with survival and reproduction, the brain has a habit of pushing us to repeat the action to obtain the reward again. But naturally, as soon as we gain the reward, we are often left feeling empty or dissatisfied.

Let's consider modern smartphone habits as an example. App developers learned that they could produce dopamine neurotransmitters by setting up apps that focus on reward-based systems. Take, for example, the likes or followers that make up social media applications. For some people, the "likes" and validation that they get on social media can release high hits of dopamine levels. In fact, many of the everyday applications we use are designed to purposefully do this. Notifications via emails, text messages, and news stories can each produce high amounts of dopamine, so we are firing off this neurotransmitter numerous times a day and expecting the same feeling each time.

Overstimulation and the Brain

Let's make one thing perfectly clear. When I say "overstimulation," I don't mean your brain is producing too much dopamine. Rather, overstimulation means that you need more external stimuli to receive the same amount of dopamine. This is the definition of overstimulation and essentially, it's what can cause addictive habits to form.

The reward system that we seek from dopamine can never be satiated in the way we want it to—in the way we *remember* it. If you have ever heard someone say that expectations can leave a person disappointed, there is quite a lot of neurological truth to that. Living in a world that is heavy with consumerism and that teaches us to search outside of ourselves for well-being and happiness means that we are in a near-constant state of overstimulation. This can have negative effects on our ability to concentrate on important tasks, engage in conversation, or even live happy, carefree lives. So, how exactly do our dopamine levels become overstimulated?

To understand overstimulation, we must look at how

this works from an addiction perspective.

The way that people become addicted to mind-altering substances has a lot to do with the disruption that occurs in the brain. When someone consumes an addictive substance over and over again, their brain becomes overstimulated and the reward pathways are disrupted. The brain now needs more external stimuli for the same amount of dopamine to be released. The brain's solution to this problem is usually one of two things: it either reduces its dopamine production or it decreases the dopamine receptors. This is why many drug or alcohol addicts will report having more of an immunity to the drug they overconsume. This is a direct result of the brain's reaction to the reward pathway being overwhelmed. The desire for drug use is still strong, but now it takes larger quantities of the drug to arrive at the same feeling.

The science behind a "dopamine detox" was developed as a way of treating patients who had overstimulation of dopamine levels due to their drug use. In modern times, we've come to understand that this overstimulation can also be experienced with everyday things such as food, sex, checking Instagram and Facebook, or going to the gym. The problem with overstimulation of dopamine levels is that the brain gets used to wanting more and more of the thing it is consuming. Engaging in activities that are centered around what the brain *expects* the reward to be can often leave us feeling demotivated afterward, as we are expecting too much of a hit and too frequently. Overstimulation can also lead to some bad habits, such as procrastination. Procrastination is caused by thoughts that tell our brain that the task is not worth the reward. The problem with dopamine is that if we are overstimulated, then the tasks that will actually bring us longer, more measured satisfaction don't seem worth it because the reward is far away.

Marketing companies and businesses alike have gained billions of dollars from collecting data that allows them to know what content we are more likely to engage with and why. Often when we are scrolling through apps such as Instagram or Facebook, we see advertisements for relevant products that we are likely to be interested in. Any time we enter a search term on the Google page, data companies collect this information. The data measure everything from how long we spend on the ad and whether we make it to checkout to the type of products we are more likely to click on. The constant side-tracking that occurs within our smartphones and computers makes the brain think that it's getting more done when in actual fact, we are almost never fully present and concentrating on one given task, which is the brain's optimal way of functioning.

Combining these dopamine-hijacking activities with our society's obsession with consumption means that overstimulation has a fairly negative impact on many people's lives. Focusing on reward-based systems can cause bad habits to form such as overspending, procrastination, overeating or drinking, and more.

The brain has a tendency to remember the feeling of pleasure or satisfaction that has been produced as greater than it actually was. In other words, overstimulation can lead to the brain expecting more of a hit than it gets. A good example of this is trying to think back to a time when you bought something online and you were greatly anticipating its arrival. When it finally arrived, you can recall a distinct difference between your *expectation* of the reward and the actual pleasure that the reward produced. The happiness that can be gained from searching for things outside of ourselves can often be fleeting and has the potential to leave us always on the lookout for the next hit.

Action Step

As the first step in your journey through this book, think about a bad habit you have had around an object or activity. Perhaps you even believe you have an addiction. Perhaps your mood, motivation, or day changes depending on whether you have this external object in the house or not. Maybe you are spending too much time on your phone. Since technology has made work, socializing, banking, shopping, and entertainment available on smartphones, most people are spending more and more time with their screen companions. Many of the apps we engage with regularly are designed to have us looking for that next dopamine hit and visiting the app more frequently. Perhaps some mornings or afternoons, you find your time swallowed up by scrolling endlessly, with little positive result. The next time you sit down to complete a task that requires direct concentration:

- Count how many times you are tempted to pick up your phone.

- Instead of giving in, simply record the number of times the thought occurs to you.

- Aim to stick with the task you are performing for at least forty-five minutes before you are allowed to check your phone.

Now, was that a difficult task for you? Did you find it difficult not to give in to your brain's desire?

Becoming aware of the distractions and the overstimulation caused by many of our daily apps can help our brains to start working on better habits.

Of course, overstimulation doesn't only come from technology. This book is going to take a deeper look into the science behind addictive substances and what actually happens to the brain when you are engaging with them. Whatever bad habit you are attempting to break, you will find advice and critical information that will help you to rewire your brain and build better habits.

Dopamine Detox—A brief summary

In this book, we will be exploring what makes people more likely to become addicted, what sort of everyday habits are causing overstimulation, and how to reset your mind so that you can live a healthier and more fulfilling life.

Let's take this opportunity to briefly explain what a dopamine detox *is* and what it *isn't*.

A Dopamine Detox Is <u>Not</u>:

A detox from dopamine.

Perhaps poorly named, a dopamine detox does not mean eliminating dopamine from your brain. In fact, this phrase was popularized when Silicon Valley tech leaders made a point of detoxing from technology for a period of time, perhaps from a couple of days up to a month or even longer. The scientific evidence that shows the negative impacts that technology can have on our brain's dopamine release is something tech CEOs are well aware of. Likely, some of the biggest tech leaders know all too well the negative impacts of overstimulation. We also know that too much exposure to blue light (from computers and phones) can reduce sleeping quality, alter moods, and generally leave people feeling a little down. But remember, it is not the dopamine that is the problem. *You are not producing more dopamine levels with overstimulation.* You are producing the same dopamine levels but need more of the external reward in order to do so. This is how cravings, bad habits, and addictions can form.

A Dopamine Detox Is

A detox from overstimulation.

A detox from overstimulation can look a little different for everyone, but the exact definition is this:

The reduction of engaging in stimulating activity in order to place you in the correct state of being to achieve life changes or goals.

The truth is, it's impossible to get exactly what we want out of life if we are letting our brains make decisions for us without investigating our habits and our thoughts. The incredible thing about being a human being—what sets us apart from other species—is the analytical mind.

19

We have the choice to be able to analyze a thought or action that we are performing and consider if it is really worth our while.

If you are tired of not getting what you want out of life and you feel like your attention is being hijacked by things that don't lead you to happiness, then a dopamine detox is exactly what you need. A lot of the activities included in this book will be combining traditional at-home methods with mindfulness methods and thought work. This is because *every action first starts as a thought.*

It is our thoughts about the external stimuli we engage in that lead to the action of overuse, which then leads to the behavior pattern. In order to tackle your bad habits and to truly break them, you must also do some thought work. We are going to get down to the nitty-gritty thoughts about the things we do every day that are not improving our quality of life. By the way, I am not just talking about smartphones here. Overstimulation and a human being's ability to become addicted to something have been around since the beginning of time. I am talking about any bad habit in your life or any obsessive thought that is causing you unhappiness. These external stimuli could be anything from:

Food

Alcohol

Cigarettes

Marijuana, prescription pills, or other drugs

Sex/Pornography

Video Games

TV apps

Work

Exercising to extremes

Coffee

Sugar

Social Media apps

All of these things can lead to overstimulation and many have been specifically *designed to do so*. Big Alcohol and

Big Tobacco created a marketing campaign that continually sought out new customers since many of their customers would suffer from short life spans as a result of their own products. The way sugar is marketed is to specifically appeal to that overstimulation in the brain, leaving us craving and wanting more. Indeed, some of our daily habits are both physically and mentally addictive. Neuroscience can teach us a lot more about this.

This book will guide you step by step to help you arrive at a better place by resetting your level of dopamine stimulation. There is nothing in this book that you will not have heard of before. This is not about throwing your smartphones and that Saturday night bottle of wine out the window. The information in this book is here to empower you and to help enhance your productivity skills.

Action Step

At this stage, you probably have a good idea of what it is that's leaving your brain wanting more and more stimulation. Whether it's overusing your phone, eating or drinking the wrong foods or beverages, porn, marijuana, working out, emails, or TikTok. The truth is that most of us are addicted to a number of things in our daily lives. Whatever it is that's causing you to be less productive, you will be able to recognize it after reading this book. For now, consider a number of daily habits that are hindering your progress. Once you have identified them, ask yourself:

● *How do I feel after engaging in this activity a number of times a day?*

● *How does this habit prevent me from getting what I need done in one day?*

● *What are changes that I can implement to help me curb this habit?*

This step is about identifying a habit that you would like to change. You are going to get very specific advice and action steps when it comes to the actual dopamine detox. But remember, it is no real use to engage with the detox if you are going to return to your bad habits as soon as the detox is over. Just as with a healthy diet, this is not about restriction or putting yourself through a sort of "punishment" only to go back to your old habits in a matter of days or weeks. This book is about educating yourself on how modern daily habits interact with your brain and how to prevent yourself from feeling the negative effects of those habits. You are going to be in a position of power because you will have a great deal of information gained from this book, so that when you have the urge to pick up your phone fifty times a day or scroll through Instagram or reach for a pack of cigarettes, you will understand 1) the danger of these habits and what they do to the brain, 2) your thoughts around these habits and how to question those thoughts, and 3) tried and tested methods that will help you reset your stimuli and return to a place of calm, serenity, balance and productivity.

Ultimately, the purpose of these methods is to help you feel your absolute best and have as much knowledge as possible about things that are hijacking your attention for the wrong reasons. Here is a brief summary of all we have learned in this chapter.

Chapter Summary

- Dopamine is a neurotransmitter that sends messages to our brain receptors that allow us to feel pleasure, motivation, and even influences our mood, behavior, and movement.

- Dopamine sends messages to our **mesolimbic reward pathway** and creates motivation within us when we think the reward is worth the effort.

- Since it rewards us for fulfilling our basic needs, such as for food and pain avoidance, dopamine is one of the main mechanisms we have to keep us alive.

- Overstimulation is not caused by your brain producing too much dopamine.

- Overstimulation means that you need more external stimuli for the same amount of dopamine.

- The reward system that we seek from dopamine can never be satiated in the way we want it to be, or in the way we *remember* it.

- When someone consumes an addictive substance over and over again, their brain becomes overstimulated and the reward pathways are disrupted.

- Overstimulation can also occur from other addictive mechanisms and activities, such as smartphones, food, and working out—essentially anything that can release large amounts of dopamine and has a pleasure reward.

- A dopamine detox does not mean detoxing from dopamine entirely.

- A dopamine detox is about resetting the amount of stimulating activity you engage in and how frequently.

- A dopamine detox has been proven to have incredible benefits, including better concentration, mood improvement, calm and serenity, and better productivity.

In the next chapter, we're going to take a look at our addiction to multitasking and why it could be harming us.

Chapter Two

Our Addiction to Multitasking

Multitasking in and of itself causes overstimulation. And guess what? We are doing it *all the time*. Essentially, when we break concentration and "indulge" in activities that are not connected to the task we are supposed to be performing, our brain considers this break from concentration a sign that we've finished what we were working on. It rewards us for this behavior by producing dopamine. Of course, an important truth about dopamine is that **the brain is never satiated by the reward it receives**. Rather, our brain gets stuck in the habit of seeking stimulation that is outside of ourselves. So, the more you break concentration to check your phone, read an article, or drink a can of soda, the more your brain wants you to do it again.

There is another problem caused by our society's obsession with multitasking. Neuroscientists and health practitioners across the world agree that our brain's cognitive ability actually *declines* when we multitask. While the dopamine release will have us thinking that we are performing better by multitasking and getting a lot done, multitasking can encourage the production of the stress hormone cortisol. This hormone reduces the brain's cognitive function. When we are stressed, we are more likely to think of tasks negatively. Negative thoughts produced from the stress response may be related to fear, which disrupts the brain's ability to function even at an average capacity. It also reduces our capability to think creatively and our openness to new ideas.

These negative thoughts are the direct result of engaging in activities that cause overstimulation of dopamine in the brain. It is in this way that *multitasking leads to procrastination*. Instead of working with the brain's ability to concentrate on one task at a time, we overwhelm ourselves and end up getting less done. If multitasking increases the stress response hormone, then the activities that we break away from are causing us more stress than happiness. But the brain can get into a looping habit of trying to do three things at once instead of taking the time to concentrate on the most important task at hand.

Multitasking is certainly an aspect of modern living. It wasn't always like this. There have been a number of significant changes to the world since the invention of the internet a mere 27 years ago. Now, it is more possible than ever to work and live remotely. Family structures have changed so that in many cases, both parents are working to support families instead of one parent remaining at home. It seems that even more has been put on our plates than ever before. During the pandemic, parents faced the responsibility of overseeing schoolwork and minding children without school, daycare, or any of the usual societal structures. Many parents were doing this while having full-time jobs and trying not to get sick at the same time. It is fair to say that the mental effects and consequences of COVID-19 on society are ongoing.

Let's take a look at the things that are causing overstimulation and the reasons behind this worldwide "burnout" feeling.

Dopamine Traps

In today's society, the things that we are addicted to are largely related to getting a dopamine release with very little effort. The truth is that millions of experts are designing platforms that exploit our brain's deep-rooted reward system. Apps, products, and content are being produced to release as much dopamine as possible in order to make us use the product over and over again. This is why social media apps display profiles based on the algorithm and not chronologically. It is the reason why online shopping outlets reward customers who come back continuously, and it is also why games have levels as well as different ranking systems in place. The idea is that we jump from one post or level or product to the next. What makes this type of behavior so easy is that the tasks at hand are not difficult to perform. The reward system is greater than the effort of the task itself. What happens when we live like this is that the activities we engage in the most are going to be low-effort, low-action, high-procrastination activities that release dopamine continuously and cause overstimulation.

Whether it is the stock market, porn, junk food, alcohol, or messaging apps, the instant gratification caused by a task that requires so little effort is the very thing that gets us addicted. We end up growing accustomed to consuming and overconsuming instead of creating. Programmers and tech developers learned that it was possible to produce dopamine from engaging with applications, as long as they were designed to do so. The dark reality of the 21st Century is that companies and billionaires profit off of our procrastination. When we engage in products that stimulate our brains and then our feelings, the profit for those companies is enormous. It is our addictive behaviors that are lining the pockets of tech, sugar, and alcohol companies, among others. It has been scientifically proven that dopamine has a direct influence on the type of decisions and actions we take. We are subconsciously focused on consuming as much as possible, instead of creating the type of lives that we envision for ourselves.

Let's look at an example.

What is the first thing you do when you wake up in the morning? Chances are—like many of us—you check your phone, scroll through the notifications that have been left overnight, perhaps read a news article or two and check some form of social media. But then what? The problem with engaging with these dopamine-releasing activities is that the result of dopamine release is for us to *want more*. When our brains associate a task with a release of dopamine, the motivation to perform that task again grows stronger, because our brain knows that it will get the reward of dopamine at the end of it. This is the cause of the problem behind the number of people that report being addicted to their phones, Netflix, or other dopamine-releasing everyday activities. From an addiction perspective, this is how dependency on drugs begins. When the brain gets used to engaging with drugs or alcohol for dopamine release, then tolerance is heightened so the user can consume more of the same drug without the release of dopamine multiplying. Now, the user needs more of the drug to feel the same amount of dopamine release, causing addiction.

The good news is that whether it is your smartphone in the morning, working late and reading emails, or watching Youtube videos, there are ways to avoid activities of overstimulation and to protect yourself from these dopamine-sucking activities, creating boundaries where they are needed.

Action Step

As part of the self-evaluation that you are performing while you read this book, find a notebook—the same one where you have written out your last action steps—and reflect on a time when you felt addicted to something that was external from yourself. Take the time to record what your life was like and how it revolved around this particular object or activity. Consider how this addiction made you feel, the ways that it impacted your life, and—if you have gotten this far—what steps you took to overcome this habit. We will return to this information later in the book. The purpose of this step is not to feel shame about the bad habits we have picked up along the way, like many fellow human beings. Rather, it is a chance to become aware of how addictive patterns can make us feel, and reflect on why it is worth fighting for balance.

Your Focus is Invaluable

Data companies are profiting from your procrastination. Have you ever considered buying a product and were then surprised to see it popping up as an ad in your news feed? Many people believe that our smartphones use their built-in microphones as a way of "spying" on us and listening to our conversations in order to target the ads we see. In actual fact, the reality is a lot more simple. Data companies such as Cambridge Analytica are a stark example of how data can be used to influence people for a political agenda. While the sneakers you were thinking of buying popping up in your news feed is not exactly political, it is certainly profitable. When Cambridge Analytica was trying to persuade undecided voters to cast their ballots for Trump, they later admitted to having over 300 data points on each user they engaged with and had a marketing budget of one million dollars a day. Day in and day out, the same people were seeing ads, videos, articles, and news stories that all centered around swaying their votes and influencing their opinions. When asked how they were able to collate so many data points, Cambridge Analytica declared that they disguised much of their data collecting as personality quizzes, such as the type that pops up on Facebook and tells us what character we are like in *Friends*. Through people willingly entering their data into these sorts of online quizzes, Cambridge Analytica was able to build a successful political campaign, courting voters with relevant, relatable content that would hijack their attention and get them to engage with the conversation. The same company was also successful in similarly persuading people in the UK to vote for Brexit.

The advancement in ad targeting and algorithms is bad news for your dopamine. The truth is, it's now more difficult than ever to stay in the present moment, focusing on the task at hand with little to no distraction. To test this, consider your morning work routine. What does it look like? If you need to get something done that requires all of your concentration, are you able to do so, or are other things constantly competing for your concentration? For example, from about 10 a.m. to

11:30 a.m., how many emails, notifications, desires to check your phone, quick Google searches, or phone calls are occurring while you're completing a specific, focused task in those 90 minutes? Now that sophisticated algorithms have a better idea as to what grabs our attention, we are competing with these companies for our own attention! The desire to click on an ad when it is exactly what you had been searching for the day before is understandably great. The problem with breaking our routine in order to attend to that irritating red notification, or to investigate the product that is being displayed to us, is that the reward system is not the same as what we imagine it to be. The motivation from the dopamine release leaves us empty in the end, especially when, after the ninety minutes have finished, you have made little progress with the task that you were supposed to be completing. You may have even spent some money on something that you weren't quite ready to buy yet. The "reward" for many of these dopamine-stealing activities is often not worth the act of breaking our concentration. Imagine trying to achieve bigger goals, such as starting a business, writing a book, or taking a college class. If our brain is used to dopamine hits day in, day out and we are trying to visualize a goal that seems too far away, then there is a big chance that our brain will tell us it's not worth it.

What is one goal in your life that you hope to achieve, but that you have always had difficulty starting or committing to? Picture that goal right now and consider the steps that you need to take in order to achieve it. For example, perhaps you have been working on a book for a number of years. You have a considerable amount of work done on the book, but you are in the in-between phase of editing what you have and deciding which parts to keep, as well as finishing the story. Not only are you trying to finish your book, but you have other priorities to take care of, such as your full-time job, any extracurricular activities, perhaps childcare or family responsibilities, and so on. When you sit down to write your book, you know that the concentration and the work that needs to be done demands your attention, perhaps in a deeper way than when you are working in your day job. What happens when you suddenly get to a difficult part in your book, or when you have been writing for a significant amount of time? What is the first thing that you are considering doing?

I am using writing as an example because it is extremely relevant when it comes to dopamine overstimulation. In order to write a book, one must practice solitude and concentrate for an extended period of time, ensuring engagement in the prefrontal cortex of the brain, in order to maintain a certain standard that is necessary for writing coherent words. Also, writing a book is a much longer process than, say, posting something on social media. With these sorts of goals, the reward can feel very far away in terms of time and other obstacles, and that reduces our brain's ability to find motivation for these tasks, even if you believe that completing such a goal will grant you deep and even lifelong satisfaction. If your brain is used to feeding itself small and continuous hits of dopamine throughout the day, there is a fair chance that your concentration levels are getting hijacked. It is during these sorts of activities, when our concentration is necessary, that the urge for dopamine stimulation can be so strong. What happens if—in the short amount of time you have carved out to work on your book—you check your phone one, two, three times, and then on the fourth time, you see something that engages your concentration more than your book, eating away at your hours and slowing the progress you have made?

It is these types of daily overstimulation habits that prevent us from getting what we want out of life and often leave us with feelings of inadequacy, dissatisfaction, and demotivation. Not only are you fighting for your concentration against billion-dollar companies, but you are also fighting against yourself!

To make things more relatable, let's take this opportunity to list some everyday activities that are stealing your concentration levels and taking control of your dopamine release.

Checking your emails: *"But checking emails is necessary!"* I hear you say. While this may be true, the fact still remains that checking emails is a way to get a hit of dopamine, perhaps during a work slog when you are avoiding the more difficult tasks that are on your plate. There is nothing wrong with email checking, providing you have a couple of hours in the day that don't include messaging back clients or colleagues. Carving out specific email-free time for yourself can help you to get more done in less time. Creating boundaries around work tasks such as emails is part of the dopamine detox that we will be studying in this book.

Checking social media pages: I understand that there may be some people reading this book who don't engage in social media, and so don't relate to this example. But think carefully here. Do you use a messaging app to communicate with friends? Do you participate in groups or events that make it necessary to engage online socially? Are there group chats you're involved in that fill your day with small bits of conversation? Whatever your involvement is with social media, the apps themselves have been designed to release dopamine when we respond to their seemingly never-ending notifications, "like" counts, and story updates. Part of the dopamine detox lifestyle is to be consistently aware of this and to put boundaries in place around our use of technology. Because this technology is still so new to many of us, these boundaries are not something we have ever been taught. It is up to you to create these boundaries and to reinforce them daily. We are going to work through ways to do that in this book.

Checking numbers: Here, I am talking specifically about investment portfolios, the stock market, even sales numbers if you are in that line of business. While there is nothing wrong with having an interest in these sorts of things, it is true that the unpredictability, as well as the possibility of a reward (if the numbers are going your way), can all cause overstimulation. If numbers aren't going your way, then there is the possibility of obsessive thinking, panic-selling, and other responses. Dedicate specific time in your day to engage with this activity, but don't let it take you away from the tasks at hand.

Snacking on high-sugar or salty foods: Now, we are not aiming to be perfectly disciplined human beings that have no faults. Most people enjoy salty or sugary foods along with a well-balanced diet. Here, it is not so much about choosing foods that are unhealthy for you, but rather it is about overindulging in foods that our bodies respond to as rewards, which will set up that cycle of needing more and more to get that dopamine release. Food cravings, as well as cigarette cravings or the urge to check our phones, can distract us from the tasks at hand and generally take up more of our brain space than we would like. In fact, scientists have noted that sugar can be as addictive as nicotine for some people. More than this, the body works best when we are physically and psychologically aligned. The food and beverages you consume have a direct influence on your mood, as well as your ability to work hard. Take note of brain-enhancing foods, breakfasts that tend to help you start your day with more energy, and lunches that don't cause an afternoon slog. We will be going through more advice on this subject later.

Watching Youtube and other video sites: It all comes down to what sort of overstimulation activities you are drawn to the most. Often, when we are in between tasks or simply when our brain decides that we need a hit of dopamine, we can get sidetracked from the task at hand and get lost in a loop of watching video after video. Sophisticated algorithms only work to tempt us even further by linking one video to the next. Instead of watching a single video on a topic of interest, we end up watching four or five. Let me make something clear: if your work requires you to engage with video content as a means of research, then that is a different thing. When these sites are used as distractions and don't benefit your knowledge or awareness of a certain topic, that's when they need to be questioned.

Thinking Long Term

When our day-to-day habit is to switch from one task to the next, and when the brain is so used to obtaining a certain level of dopamine, it can be difficult to see how it's possible to ever arrive at real and genuine success. Many successful people will tell you that consistency is one of the most important steps when it comes to achieving what you want out of life. But, when our attention is constantly being ripped away from us, it can be difficult to focus on those long-term goals, and we wonder if we will ever get there.

One thing that is sometimes overlooked when it comes to overstimulation is the kinds of *thoughts* that distraction, procrastination and multitasking can cause. Not only are we left wanting more of the reward when we engage in these activities, but they can lead to a lot of self-criticism and self-doubt, especially when we are trying to find the motivation to work on those larger goals, the ones that demand more of our time and concentration than we are used to giving. If your motivation is stuck in overstimulation activities— actions that do not serve your higher purpose or move you closer to your goals—then before you know it you have given away hundreds of hours on activities that don't serve you. The thoughts that follow when we are in the habit of engaging in these dopamine-producing activities can be just as damaging.

This book has an entire chapter dedicated to thought work—questioning the thoughts around the activities that are causing your distraction and learning how to build yourself up to achieve what you really want in life. Every action begins as a thought. Nothing has been brought into this world without the first initial thought from the person who created the idea or realized the need for such a thing. If you are wondering why you haven't gotten where you need to be yet, then consider those daily habits, the daily distractions, and how they make you feel. Let's return to the writing analogy and imagine that you are constantly distracted by your smartphone during the time you have carved out to write your book. Some thoughts that you might be associating with that writing task now could look something like this:

"I can't keep concentration for long enough to make real progress."

"I always get distracted with my phone and my time is eaten away."

"Maybe I just don't have the drive or the discipline to write."

"I must not be good enough at writing. That's why I am always distracted."

"My brain just isn't able to be as productive as I need it to be."

If you insert your own goal in place of the example of writing a book, do these self-deprecating thoughts look familiar to you? If so, I am here to tell you that you are *more than capable of achieving your goals.* In fact, I believe that you can achieve anything that you set your mind to. It doesn't matter how many times you think you have failed, or how out of sync you feel with your daily habits. The fact of the matter is that you are working on yourself by reading this book and by choosing to investigate some things in your life that aren't serving you the way that you need them to.

With the negative, dissatisfying feeling that can often follow a dopamine-infused activity binge, it is no wonder that you are left with little confidence in yourself. But I am here to tell you that you have control over every single one of your thoughts, feelings, and actions. Just because you haven't quite gotten into the groove of where you need to be productivity-wise does not mean that you can't get there. This journey is going to require not just investigating your daily habits, but also investigating some of the negative thoughts you may unknowingly hold about the activities that could lead to you finally opening that business, working on that project, or saving money for a house. If you have been struggling with getting where you want to be in your life, then we will need to make sure that the thoughts you have around goal-building and productivity are positive, self-building, and not laced in self-hate and blaming. Regardless of where you are on your journey, the potential of even one human being is incredible. When the human brain sets its mind on something incredible, things can happen.

Action Step:

Now that you have reflected on some poor daily habits, as well as something you have felt addicted to before, it is time to focus on your goals.

Take this moment to consider some of the key goals that you are committed to achieving in the next five years. Get very specific here—the more specific and visual you are about your goals, the more likely it is that you will work toward achieving them.

Look at each goal one at a time and consider some of the tasks you will need to perform in order to move forward. While you list the required tasks for each goal, define whether each task is a *daily*, *weekly*, or *ongoing* task.

For example, if your goal is to increase your salary within the next year, then some of the required tasks could look something like this:

- Schedule a specific time to improve qualifications and apply for jobs. (daily, weekly)

- Gain skill in a field of expertise: studying,

advancing knowledge. (ongoing, weekly)

- Get the most out of the hours that work best for me/Analyze when I do my best work. (daily)

- Generate my own clients by setting aside time for my business. (daily, weekly)

- Present new job ideas that I could do for the company I work for, encouraging promotion. (ongoing)

Make sure to check in with yourself about how you are feeling when you write down the tasks you need to perform to achieve your goal. Do you find it overwhelming to think about your long-term goals and what will be expected of you? Perhaps you even felt an urge to reach for a distraction while making this list. Whatever emotions come up, don't worry. We are going to be learning how you can create positive, productive thoughts to help you move toward your goals. We will come back to this list later in the book, so keep your action steps in the same notebook to refer to later.

Let's look at a quick recap of everything we discussed in

this chapter:

Chapter Summary

- Multitasking may be doing you more harm than good.

- The brain does not know the difference between tasks that *are* good for us and tasks that *feel* good to us. Dopamine overstimulation allows the brain to "reward" itself for bad behavior.

- Neuroscientists and health practitioners across the world agree that our brain's cognitive ability actually *declines* when we multitask.

- Instead of working with the brain's ability to concentrate on one task at a time, we overwhelm ourselves and end up getting less done.

- Billion-dollar companies are taking advantage of your brain. Many experts are designing platforms that exploit our brain's deep-rooted reward system.

● What makes this type of behavior so easy is that these dopamine-producing tasks are not difficult to perform.

● Daily boundaries implemented around the things that are causing overstimulation will be an essential step toward freedom.

● Data companies are profiting from your procrastination. It is up to you to take back control.

● If you feel constantly tired, lethargic, demotivated, and stuck in a rut, it could be because of dopamine overstimulation.

● Engaging in instant gratification tasks such as checking emails, messaging apps, entertainment sites, and eating high-processed foods can make important goals seem more unreachable and unattainable.

● Daily habits that are centered around the goals you

wish to achieve will be greatly helped by eliminating distractions and anything that causes overstimulation.

● In order to get what you want out of life, you need to start building daily habits and routines that are aligned with your goals.

● Obsessive thinking, resistance, fear, and anxiety are all reasons why people don't go after what they really want in life.

● Overstimulation can cause many people to ignore their greater goals and get stuck in a never-ending cycle of reward-based, low-energy, and low-motivation tasks.

● Society is focused on overconsumption as opposed to creation. Instead of building a life around consuming as much as possible, this book will help you step onto the path of creating and staying consistent in working toward your goals so that you can finally get more done and gain long-lasting satisfaction.

CHAPTER THREE

Dopamine Detox Explained

The Constant Loop of Instant Gratification

Known as the chemical of want and desire, scientists and neurologists agree that dopamine and our body's interaction with this neurotransmitter has a lot to do with our likelihood of survival. Ever wonder why it feels so good to do things like have sex or eat a large steak? The pleasure experienced during sex is connected to the purpose of human reproduction. Similarly, our body sees a fatty piece of meat as critical for our survival. Without greater context, our body sees these and other dopamine-releasing activities as ways of staying alive.

While the brain responds to things that are pleasurable, it doesn't always consider which things are better for us. If you are faced with a salad or a hamburger, your brain will want to choose the hamburger over the healthier option. (I recognize that not everyone likes hamburgers—insert your own guilty pleasure food for reference!) This is because it recognizes the pleasure associated with eating something that may not be particularly good for us. The possibility of dopamine release is enough motivation to have you seeking the unhealthier option, at least until you analyze that thought. Now, most of the time, you may engage with your analytical mind and make a decision based on what you know to be true. For example, *"I had a hamburger yesterday, so I don't need one today,"* or, *"I tend to get more work done in the afternoon when I eat lighter."* But if you've gotten into the habit of choosing instant gratification over choices that will serve you better long-term, then you may be stuck in a loop of seeking gratification and pleasure over what is actually good for you. Dopamine does not know what is good for us and what is not so good for us. All that dopamine is seeking is the potential for pleasure. It does not consider the context in which we are finding that pleasure. This is why addicts find themselves in hopeless cycles of getting a hit again and again.

From the action steps that you have already performed, you should have a fair idea of what sort of daily habits you are engaging in that are counter-active. At this stage, you have reflected on some ways you have created these poor habits, the reasons why these habits are so appealing to the brain but so damaging to the psyche, and you have reflected on one substance in particular that you have felt addicted to. That substance could be alcohol or it could be something as simple as a family-sized chocolate bar every night. Whatever it is, you have recognized that there are certain overstimulation activities that you engage in—just like everyone else—that are affecting your overall productivity. Finally, from the action steps we have covered so far, you should have visualized a goal that you are ready to move toward. You should have an idea of the sort of daily, weekly, and ongoing tasks that are necessary for you to put that goal into action. Before you focus on implementing these tasks into your routine, as well as weakening some of the negative habits, you are going to perform a dopamine detox.

How To Prepare for a Dopamine Detox

The first thing to learn about a dopamine detox is that there are many different ways to do one! There are no hard and fast rules that say you need to detox for seven days, or that you must also include a fast from food. The only requirement necessary to perform a dopamine detox is a well-executed plan that fits in with your schedule and does not negatively impact your responsibilities. Obviously, it's not convenient for you to perform a dopamine detox for 72 hours if you depend on social media for your revenue and you are scheduled to post a certain amount of content in that time. Having said that, if your job is tech-heavy, then it is probably even more necessary for you to take a break from screens than if your job doesn't require daily screen time. But it is understandable that for some people, it's hard to imagine being able to "disappear" for a certain amount of time. That is why it's important to have a realistic and strategic plan in place *before* you detox.

Depending on what type of detox you are performing, you will need to arrange your schedule so that you have a certain amount of uninterrupted dopamine downtime. Remember, a dopamine detox is not about detoxing from dopamine entirely. The process made popular by Silicon Valley techies is poorly named—it is more about catchy alliteration than scientific accuracy. So no, you're not detoxing from dopamine, nor should you ever detox entirely from this important neurotransmitter. Rather, you are detoxing from or reducing dopamine-stimulant activities such as messaging apps, engaging with emails, screen time, junk food, entertainment or music, and essentially anything that can cause a spike in dopamine levels for you.

The purpose of a dopamine detox is not to starve yourself of the things that you enjoy, but rather to perform a crucial brain activity that will help strengthen your concentration and productivity in the long run. The purpose is also to reset your dopamine levels and to help you get to a place where you are not constantly reaching for the next push notification, online shopping cart, or news story. Detoxing from activities on which we mindlessly spend hours each day helps people find their true purpose in life and experience the long-term joy of achieving their goals. In order to ensure your success the first time around, let's consider some of the things that you will need to do before you start your detox.

1. Inform your friends, colleagues, and family about your brief hiatus from the online world. This step will look different for everyone. If your livelihood is wrapped up in engaging with screens and applications, then ensure that you are performing this detox at a time when you can take a break from work. Whether that means completing work in advance or taking some time off, or whether that simply means performing the detox on the weekend, make sure that there are no pressing concerns that you need to worry about and no possibility of creeping onto the laptop to check your email. If you intend to do the detox, then you might as well do it right.

2. Prepare your phone for the detox. This may seem like an obvious step, or it may seem extreme to others, but I'm strongly encouraging you to delete all social media and messaging apps from your phone before starting the detox. The old saying says that the less willpower required to perform a task, the more likely it is to get done. Don't make things harder for yourself, especially since you know that your brain has a pattern of driving you to open that social media app for a dopamine hit. Make sure that you have all of your passwords and log-in credentials before deleting the applications themselves. Take the time to eliminate all distractions.

3. Let anyone you live with or who you share office space with know that you are performing this detox. Some things can't be helped, such as whether you hear the buzz of a television nearby or whether your neighbors have a habit of cranking up their music at night. But just like during meditation, try to build a quiet space that allows you to do the things you need to do and not become too stressed about anything you can't

control. If you are living with people and you are performing your detox at home, then it is no harm to pass this information on to your roommate or partner. Most people will be respectful and even interested in what you are doing, and may make certain adjustments for one or two days.

4. Tie up any loose ends BUT don't let this step become an excuse for avoiding a dopamine detox in the first place! If you are in the process of generating new clients for a business, or if you're waiting to hear about a certain job application, then the thought of doing a dopamine detox even for one day might seem risky. But don't let the strong grip that tech has over us prevent you from ever taking a break. If you have a high-pressure job, you could forward your incoming mail to someone you trust who can take on the responsibility of dealing with your workload for a short period of time. This step is somewhat connected to the first step. No matter how hectic and crazy your schedule is, a dopamine detox is not something that is designed to last forever, so it's important to maintain the time allocated for

the detox and to cover your tracks based on your usual tech-focused responsibilities.

5. Set an intention or a goal for your dopamine detox. This can be based on a mantra that you believe in, a thought that you are trying to break away from, or it could be a bigger goal that you are preparing to work on. Whatever your reason for performing the detox, make sure that it is true and important to you. Holding this intention in your mind during times when temptation is knocking on your door will help you to stay motivated and focused. Make sure that the intention is something that is clear and that makes sense to you, as well as something that feels meaningful. If you want to feel happier day to day, then your intention might look something like, "I am committed to long-term happiness over instant gratification." Focus your mind on what the thing that you are craving actually does to your brain and how it usually ends up making you feel. When we quit something or when we are trying to form new habits, the brain will think of creative ideas to avoid this. Fight against your negativity

bias and stay focused on your intention. This will help you to see success.

What Am I Detoxing From?

When you are used to performing tasks based on an empty reward system, your brain has created a pattern of thinking that is hindering your progress. The solution is to *remove things that cause overstimulation*. Depending on what type of detox you are going to perform, here is a list of things that you may be detoxing from for a short period of time.

Social Media

Create realistic barriers such as deleting the apps on your phone and if necessary, changing your password and entrusting it to someone else, so that you are sure no temptations will arise. Password changes and even deletion of apps may not be necessary. But when you are preparing for the dopamine detox, make sure that you are very honest with yourself. The less temptation there is around you, the easier this detox will be. Any apps or websites that facilitate communication with friends or others, as well as image-based apps such as Pinterest, should be out of use during your dopamine detox. If you depend on Instagram or another app for your income, don't allow that to prevent you from engaging in the detox. Perhaps it will work for you to have a shorter detox, say for 24 hours. Regardless of how long you choose to withdraw, ensure that you have mentally and practically prepared yourself to be uncontactable online during this time. Tell your friends not to worry and that you'll be back soon. Aside from the people that you interact with every day, you may be surprised at how little you miss your phone during this time.

Digital Entertainment

Digital entertainment refers to Netflix or other video accounts, plus any video games or devices that you play games with. If you are performing this dopamine detox because you feel addicted to any of these devices, such as your PlayStation or the newest version of Fifa, then it might seem daunting to give it up cold turkey. But just remember the rules from the last section. Prepare your living space so that temptations are nowhere near you.

It's just like when someone wants to cut out fatty foods—when it's not in the house, it requires a lot less willpower. You can have fun while you perform these preparation tasks! Lock up the PlayStation in the trunk of your partner's car. If it's something that you have had arguments over, no doubt your partner will happily help you hide the temptation! If you live with others and the idea of removing all digital entertainment around you seems difficult, then map out exactly where you will be spending your detox. We will walk through daily plans and advice on how to spend your time during your detox later in the book. If you are house sharing, it would be a great idea to make your room a pleasant place to be for long amounts of time. Spend the time wisely by getting an early night's sleep or doing some light and non-stimulating reading (we'll get into what that means later). Prepare yourself for the peace and quiet of this digital break. It's worth noting that during this time, you will be performing mental practices such as meditation. While you take this "time out," you may discover that you find the answer to a nagging question, or you may realize that you are just one thought away from advancing yourself in your business. The thoughts that form after a dopamine detox are clearer, more balanced, and often a lot more productive. The quiet downtime that you are going to experience during your detox will all come back to serve you in a positive way. So, for now, say goodbye to the digital distractions.

Junk Food

We are talking about junk food here, not because a dopamine detox has anything to do with a diet, but because *food greatly influences how we feel emotionally and physically.* In fact, nowadays, soybeans are genetically modified, vegetables and fruits are often sprayed with pesticides and treated with chemicals, and meats are pumped with hormones. It can be a difficult challenge to ensure that your family and loved ones are eating nutritious and trustworthy food. Junk food is obviously a huge dopamine stimulant for many reasons. The sugar, fat, and salt that we put into our bodies signals to our brains that this is part of our survival, so we must eat as much as possible—similar to the scavenger mindset. If you have lost control of your eating habits and tend to eat a lot of sugary and salty foods at night, then you are not alone. The detox is not meant to blame or cause shame, but cutting out chips, sodas, unhealthy chocolate (as in, chocolate that is less than 80% cacao), and sugary drinks, is essential for having a successful detox. There have been people who have chosen to fast entirely for the 24 hours of a dopamine detox. From the reports that I have read, most people who engage in a full-on food fast tend to be so overwhelmed with the natural desire to eat that they can't enjoy or appreciate the detox for what it is. My advice to you would be to *focus on the obviously stimulating foods.* Dopamine that is released from normal foods we eat is not the same as the dopamine that is released from unhealthy foods. As we know by now, the problem with dopamine-enhancing foods and activities is that it leaves the person wanting more. There are obvious negative impacts to eating a large amount of sugar and salt every single night while sitting in front of the TV. And by now you will have done the work to reflect on what things you are most addicted to. But food is necessary and essential. Personally, I think it is more important to eliminate the things that cause overstimulation rather than cutting out food altogether. But it is entirely up to you! Take on what you know you can handle. Then when you perform your next detox, you will be better prepared, knowing what to expect.

Drink

Only water. This sounds a lot harder than it is. If you, like me, are a coffee fiend and function only with two to three cups per day, then the idea of cutting out coffee even for one day can be daunting. But if the very idea of taking a 24-hour break from coffee fills you with dread, then that probably means the break will do you some good. Caffeine does give us a burst of dopamine, so interacting with coffee while on a dopamine detox may be counter-productive. Also, it is a good challenge to use the time that you are detoxing to evaluate all of your habits and to make sure that you are engaging with reward systems that are really valuable! Again, there is nothing wrong with feeling good after performing a certain task or activity. But many of our tasks and habits are performed subconsciously with very little thought of how they are impacting our larger goals, aspirations, and happiness. If your goal is to feel less anxious or depressed or to improve your mood in general, then I would definitely suggest you consider including coffee in this detox. Caffeine impacts our mood, sleep pattern, and anxiety levels, so taking a break, even if just for 24 hours, can only be a good thing. The purpose of the dopamine detox is to remove all pleasure-seeking activities from your brain for this certain span of time. This is not to "punish" you but rather, to help reset your stimulation level and to help you enjoy life even more than before. See how you feel after drinking only water for this time.

Alcohol and Drugs

This may seem like a fairly obvious one, but chances are there are many people reading this book who use alcohol and drugs, perhaps daily. Whether you are consuming medical marijuana, drinking one or two glasses of wine a night, or relying on getting obliterated every weekend to keep work stress at bay, consuming anything that is a mind-altering substance is a definite no for a dopamine detox. However, if you have, or believe you may have, a chemical dependency on alcohol or drugs, you will need a different approach. For you, it is extremely important to seek a doctor's help and advice before abstaining from alcohol or drugs.

Remember too that *alcohol is the only drug where death is possible from stopping cold turkey.* So, if you believe that you have a problem with alcohol and that quitting even for 24-48 hours may have a serious impact on you, then you need to seek medical help before performing any kind of detox. The kind of detox we're focused on here involves the everyday habits we have that will hang us up and distract us from our goals. It is true that this form of detox is related to addiction methods for rehabilitation centers. However, this is not the same thing as quitting a highly-addictive and dangerous substance. Doing anything of the sort must always be monitored by a professional. Also, if you take medication as prescribed by your doctor, then of course, you should continue to take this medication during the detox. For the casual in-between users, I recommend taking a break and—depending on how long you are detoxing—eliminating temptations around the house in the same way that you would with food.

Pornography

In fact, it's a good idea to eliminate all sexual activity during this dopamine detox. Our brains think of sex as an act of reproduction that keeps our species alive, so it makes sense that they can go crazy with desire and enjoy it so much. Obviously, there is nothing wrong with enjoying sex! But it's important to do this detox properly and to eliminate every dopamine-stimulant activity.

Music

If you're thinking that this is going to be too much for you, don't give up before you start! It may seem a little daunting, reading all of the "don'ts" one after another. But the purpose of this list is not to scare you off or make you feel like you can't do it. It's important to consider what each activity does to your psyche and why it could be bringing about overstimulation. Music is a wonderful gift and there is a lot to be said for the way concentration levels improve while listening to certain types of music, such as jazz or classical. But we run the risk in modern times of never experiencing moments of silence or solitude, consistently seeking out the next dopamine hit. While listening to music as you're working or getting ready isn't the same as playing four hours of video games a night, it should still be minimized or completely absent during the days that you are detoxing. The goal of this detox is to bring you to a state of mind where you are feeling more ready than ever to work on your goals. Keeping the goal in mind will help you during this time of silence. So many human beings are scared of being alone with their own thoughts. This is not something that we should ignore. If this is difficult for you, then you have the opportunity and the power to change this! You do not have to be constantly distracted or ignoring things that cause you stress. Consider some thought work methods that you can use during the dopamine detox, which we will examine in detail later in the book. It's good to be comfortable with just our own company.

Reading and Socializing

Communication should be kept to a minimum, which includes reading or talking. Communicating with people gives us a hit of dopamine—which is perfectly fine—but for this exercise you are avoiding all things that produce dopamine for a short period of time. Reading can be performed during a dopamine detox and we can talk about exactly what type of reading I am referring to a little later.

Emails, The Stock Market, Finance-Related Numbers

I remember my first job at a busy tech company. A lot of the middle and upper management would talk about the constant flow of emails coming through their inboxes. I remember feeling anxious about my measly five to ten emails per day when I had just started, trying to double up on communication so that it felt like I was working more. It seemed that the more important you were, the more overwhelmed with emails you became. There was an almost boastful tone when it came to comparing email loads, especially when an important person had taken some time off work or—God forbid—even enjoyed a vacation. Important employees would swap stories of when they couldn't even find the time to respond to their emails with jobs that had them on call pretty much 24/7. Some would choose to work from home, others would sit in a different part of the building where no one could find them, and some would wear noise-canceling headphones that signaled they were not to be disturbed. Whatever your situation is at work with communication and the constant stream of never-ending availability, the dopamine detox may be exactly what you need to assert some boundaries. If you are someone who has a high-paying job that requires you to have customer-facing meetings, then there is no reason why you couldn't hand off your emailing tasks to an assistant or copywriter that you trust. Sometimes, especially if the business we are working in is our own, we can get caught up in thinking that we need to do everything or else it won't get done properly. Not only is this a counter-productive way to work, but it is also exhausting!

If you have too much on your plate, trying to respond to your clients at the same time as trying to onboard new clients while all the while older clients are shouting about not getting enough attention, then something has to change. No matter what type of position you have, there should be at least one person whom you trust to take over your tasks when you are not around to manage them, or when you require some time off. Everyone— no matter how important or seemingly insignificant their job title—needs time off. The dopamine detox you are about to begin is exactly that. It will allow you to take a break, sit back, and think about nothing for a moment.

It is about clearing your mind and your muscle memory of all of the daily habits that consume you and that seem never-ending. This space can have powerful effects on the mind. Especially when teamed up with meditation and thought work, a dopamine detox has the ability to give you a totally new perspective on your life. You will see in Chapter Six, "An Introduction to Meditation," how quieting the mind and practicing mindfulness can allow for clearer, more productive thoughts—thoughts that get you from A to B to C a lot more quickly than before.

Okay, so emails are one thing. But what about other daily habits you feel you need to stay on top of—such as the stock market—and making sure that those numbers are where they need to be? Trust me; I understand how addicting the stock market can be. When I started training, I had an alarm set for when the markets would open—as if I needed the reminder! If you are engaging in a longer detox but are afraid about what will happen to your positions, there are a couple of things you can do.

First of all, unless you are a stockbroker, have some sort

of mathematics degree, or are specifically working in this industry, then chances are you are not the best person to be leveraging and managing your stock. I know that might be hard to read! There has been a keen interest in the stock market over the past couple of years. Cryptocurrency, tech stocks, and electric vehicle stocks, for example, have attracted a mass following of people interested in investing their money and seeing a profit. As someone who has friends that work in the stock market, as well as someone who engages in the stock market myself, this is what I have learned when it comes to dopamine and stocks.

You need to be honest with yourself about your purpose when engaging with the stock market in an obsessive or addictive manner. Are you honest with yourself about your stock expertise, or are you just looking to get a hit of adrenaline, similar to when a high bet is placed on a baseball team? With a constant and ever-changing world, one disaster after the next, and mass media coverage of it all, there is certainly risk. But there are very pragmatic and independent ways that you can tackle this addiction.

First of all, if you are *not* someone who has directly studied finance, extensively worked as a stockbroker, or has a suitable degree, then consider having a stock broker manage your portfolio for you. Too often, people are obsessively making changes to their stock portfolio, losing money unexpectedly, and then trying to fix it by investing more money that they don't have. Engaging in the stock market in this way is no different from gambling. If you are really looking to get away from your responsibilities, especially for a longer period, such as the three- to seven-day detox, then consider finding someone to be that replacement for you. This can be a professional stockbroker, an assistant or colleague who can manage your clients, or even a friend who promises to answer your business phone for an hour or two. Whatever you need to do to get some space from those things that are robbing your attention and your dopamine, do it. Make the necessary arrangements so that on the first day of your detox you are waking up confident and ready to be mentally untethered to those daily responsibilities.

But How?

So now that you know what sort of dopamine-sensitive things you should be avoiding, you may be thinking to yourself, *"How am I going to do this?"* If you have ever lived in a rural town, you may know what it is like to be in complete darkness at a certain time of night. In many rural towns, even the nearest street light is a couple of miles down the road. When it gets dark, it gets really dark! Of course, there are huge benefits to this. For one, your circadian rhythm thrives on being able to have a good night's sleep with a blackened sky. And of course, if you go deep into the country where it isn't littered with city lights, you will be able to see the stars a lot more clearly. You may even be able to stargaze and catch meteor showers. Consider your dopamine detox like a small trip to the countryside. This is a brain habit that will revert you back to a time when you were not dependent on so much dopamine throughout the day. If you find it difficult, that is perfectly normal. It is a brain activity that many people prefer to ignore. But the goal of this exercise is to put attention on your long-term goals, long-term happiness, and achieve a more fruitful and happier life. It is not the goal to totally disengage from technology forever. In fact, it is up to you how long you perform this detox. Below are some dopamine detox timeframes you can try. Take a look at their descriptions and start considering which detox suits your schedule, needs, and responsibilities the most.

24-hour Dopamine Detox

A 24-hour dopamine detox is not going to cause too much upheaval in your life. Most people, no matter how important or digitally available they usually are, can carve out one single day when they omit any dopamine-stimulant activities. If you have children, a high-pressure job, or if you are struggling with the addictive use of any of the substances above, then a 24-hour detox is a great way to start.

The benefits of a 24-hour dopamine detox are multifold. It gives you a really good idea of what to expect if you want to do this again. It won't disrupt your schedule too much. Choose a lazy Saturday or Sunday to start off your detox and plan the day according to what you are going to do—but remember, the aim is to do as few stimulating activities as possible. The day might stretch out a little longer than usual, and you may spend some time twiddling your thumbs and planning which low-stimulating activity to do next. But remember, once you have your intention firmly in place in your mind, you should be able to see even slight boredom or the passing temptation as part of the fun. If you start the detox at 10 p.m. the evening before, then you will feel almost giddy at ten to ten the next night. But this is not a high from the desire to consume foods or check your phone. Rather, it's pride that you have survived the day, despite your brain's temptations, and not given in to instant gratification.

It is true that a 24-hour dopamine detox will not reset your dopamine overstimulation as much as a lengthier amount of time like a 48-hour detox. But if time or your schedule are issues for you, then 24 hours is the perfect way to dip your toe into the water. Once you've done it one time, it will feel less strange to pick up this healthy habit once a month, and so on. Overall, a 24-hour detox is a great starting point and you should certainly be proud of yourself for engaging in this brain exercise.

48-hour Dopamine Detox

A 48-hour detox is going to be twice —or half —as demanding as the 24-hour detox. It depends on how you look at it! Some find that they prefer the additional time to get into the detox and the new mental habits. It can be a quiet, still time full of reflection and introspection. But try not to get lost in your thoughts.

A 48-hour detox will demand more from you, your brain, your commitment, and your concentration levels. It can also be done on a weekend and with little interruption to your normal life. If you are part of a family, then this can be a great partial detox to do together. Okay, you may not end up sitting in silence for the whole day if young children are around. But if the aim is to simply coax them off their screens and into nature, then a trip to the countryside or even a camping site can be great. Stepping outside of your environment, both physically and habitually, can be equally helpful. Taking in refreshing scenery is a great way to enhance a new set of habits, even if just for two days. Take some friends, a partner, a cat, or even better, yourself, and treat the detox as a way to decompress and to allow yourself to unplug.

Remember to keep your intention at the forefront of the 48-hour detox. In the next chapter, we will go through some day plan ideas, temptations to expect, and some mindful activities to integrate into your routine.

Three to Seven Day Dopamine Detox

For those of you who are really looking to reset your dopamine receptors, the three to seven-day dopamine detox is for you. However, there is a likelihood that anyone who is performing a seven-day dopamine detox may have a certain amount of screen and work commitments to uphold. You may need to collect kids from school or conduct meetings at work. For those that want to blend a dopamine detox in with your normal lifestyle, the partial dopamine detox allows for this. But some will also choose to set their weeks up to eliminate *all* dopamine-stimulant tasks and commit to a longer stint. The three- to seven-day dopamine detox will uphold the same practices as the 24- and 48-hour detox. The difference is in the length of time and, as a result of this, the endurance and stamina needed. Committing to a three- to seven-day dopamine detox, even if it is a partial dopamine detox (allowing for essential screen time, communication, responsibilities, etc.) will allow for a greater reset of overstimulation. But that doesn't necessarily mean that the temptations won't creep in. There is a famous saying in neuroscience that goes, *"Neurons that fire together wire together"*. This is absolutely true for all of our daily habits and the way the brain works on muscle memory. In the chapter "Post-Detox Daily Habits," we will take a detailed look at how to break some of those thought habits so that your dopamine detox will be more manageable, and so you have a real shot at creating some life-fulfilling habits that will lead to greater success, happiness, and peace of mind.

Check In With Your Brain

So, we've gone through all of the different "essential" habits that you are going to give up during your dopamine detox. Seeing all of these items in a list—the very things that you have identified as the focus of your own addictive tendencies—may be overwhelming. In fact, if your brain is doing its job, then it is probably thinking of some creative, new reasons that prove that this is all just a terrible idea, the addictions in your life are not as bad as you think they are, and you should just shut this book right now and go have a cigarette, a soda, or scroll through your phone. Don't worry. This is the brain's natural reaction to things. You see, it likes to get out of doing "new" things. In fact, the brain cares more about being right than it does about how you feel. Again, as the old saying goes, neurons that fire together wire together. Your body is so used to being on auto-pilot and doing the things that enable dopamine release that *not* doing these things, even for 24 hours, may seem daunting.

This is why it's important to engage with your analytical mind and not allow your body and your brain to simply decide things for you, without closer inspection. Of course, the reality is that you are spending hours, weeks, and years of your life performing tasks that are not related to self-development or to getting what you truly want out of life. In fact, most tasks are related to *not* doing something. How many times have you considered working on your business, going through your finances, studying a subject that intrigues you or setting up a dating app that you've spent months thinking about? If you're frustrated with yourself, confused as to why your brain always tends to go to your phone or the snack aisle instead of doing something that will bring you greater happiness, then don't be. The brain has recognized that your indulgent habits have faster reward systems. But here's the thing. Your brain is viewing those rewards as worthy—as worth having—when in actual fact, the reward is simply that hit of dopamine. And because the reward does not actually equate to real, genuine progress, you are left with that all-too-familiar feeling of emptiness, of wondering where the time went and why you find it so hard to work on the things you care about. You might even have self-depreciating thoughts. *"I must not want x enough, otherwise, I would work on it more!" "I am never going to find a partner because I don't bother to put in the effort,"* or *"Maybe I am not destined to be successful. Maybe I don't have the strength to do this."*

I am here to tell you that your destiny is as great as you

can imagine it to be! Everything that has ever entered this world first began as a thought.

What are some predisposed ideas that you have about the things you want, the things that take effort, that may be preventing you from getting started? Let's use searching for your dream job as an example. Everyone deserves to work in a job they love and yet this is still a new concept to some people—something that seems out of reach. Your work situation will be influenced by a lot of things: the type of family you have, whether you support loved ones, whether you are an able-bodied person, what type of education you have had, etc.

But time and time again, we have found examples of people who have soared beyond their supposed limitations and done incredible things. One such notable person was Stephen Hawking, who was one of the greatest minds known to mankind. Hawking was a theoretical physicist, cosmologist, and author. He also lived with Lou Gehrig's disease, which is a motor neuron disease that impacts the physical movement and functioning of the body. Despite this, Stephen Hawking used his mind and brain to achieve incredible results and advancements in the world of science.

Now, imagine if Stephen Hawking's mind had told him over and over that he would not be able to achieve certain things in life due to his autoimmune system? I think it is fair to say that the universe would be worse off because of it.

Another example is the renowned composer Beethoven, who gradually became deaf over a number of years before completely losing his sense of hearing at age 45. Although this was obviously a huge difficulty for Beethoven, he continued to compose music without being able to hear. In fact, he even reflected his struggles and difficulty with deafness in some of his later compositions. A strong example of a more melancholic style of Beethoven's work can be found in his Sixth Symphony (California Symphony, 2020).

Regardless, the work that Beethoven composed while deaf is nothing short of stupendous. The emotion and human experience that he was able to reflect within his music may not have had the impact it did had it not been for his physical impairment. Imagine if Beethoven had told himself that he could never compose again once he became deaf?

Both Hawking and Beethoven are examples of how powerful the mind can be when we are persistent in believing that we are capable of doing anything that we want.

Predisposed, negative, and subconscious thoughts about not ever having your dream job or work situation may look something like this:

- "In order to earn money, I must work in a job that is not my passion."

- "I have to work nine hours a day, five days a week. Otherwise, I won't be able to make enough money."

- "I barely make ends meet with my current job."

- "I am not educated or skilled enough to get the job I really want."

- "I need to work in an office job, even though I hate working in an office."

- "Most people with my experience don't earn much money."

- "Everyone feels like this so I just need to suck it up."

- "I don't think I'm valuable or skilled enough to work in the job that I really want."

Consider how you can start to challenge some of these thoughts and turn them around to mean the opposite of what you subconsciously believe.

We are going to get into more detail about thought work in the chapter called "Post-Detox Daily Habits," but for now, dedicate some time to identifying and then questioning some thoughts you have about starting your dopamine detox. Perhaps you're doubtful that you can find time in your schedule to even give it a try. Maybe all of your responsibilities and tech-related tasks are adding up in your mind. Maybe the thought of waking up without coffee, even for one day, seems like torture. Or perhaps you are genuinely struggling with addictive behaviors around one or more of the stimuli listed and you don't know if you can do it.

First of all, this detox can be done to suit your needs and schedule. Also, there is nothing wrong with being honest with yourself and identifying some resistant feelings you have toward getting started. In the next chapter, we are going to focus on all of the things you can do during your dopamine detox, and in Chapter Five, we'll discuss what a partial dopamine detox looks like, which can still be massively helpful.

Action Step

Write down three thoughts you have that are based on resistance to the dopamine detox. You can be as negative or as critical as you like. These thoughts may look something like this:

"This is dumb—I bet it doesn't even work."

"Everyone spends their time on social media. It's the 21st Century. I don't need a break."

"I can't do it, so there isn't much point in trying."

"I'll never be able to find the time. And if I can't do it properly, then what's the point?"

Human beings have to work really hard not to let negative thoughts get the better of them. Negative thoughts are *30 times* more likely to stick in our minds than positive ones. This is why we were designed with an analytical mind. The subconscious mind thinks up to 30,000 thoughts per day. And if our brain is more likely to pay attention to negative thoughts, it's no wonder we find it so hard to be happy sometimes. Trying to seek happiness from outside of ourselves—from the TV, a bottle of wine, or "likes" on an Instagram photo—does not lead to true fulfillment. As mentioned before, when you hear those negative, resistant thoughts, they have more to do with the design of our brains than how you actually feel. If you've recognized that you have a problem or you feel the negative impacts of some of your daily activities, then you have already made up your mind. You have already decided that you want to change habits in your life in order to be happier and more productive. But as we know, the brain doesn't like to be wrong. And it can take some time to really change our thoughts. Actually, there is a lot of thought work and checking in with yourself that are necessary throughout this process. So—without being self-critical—try to reshape some of those thoughts that are wrapped up in resistance and procrastination. You don't have to saturate these thoughts with false positivity, but you can find a more neutral ground to build the new thought on. You can choose how you feel about taking this step to create better habits for yourself and removing dopamine-stimulant substances, even if for a couple of days. Here are some examples as to what those new and improved thoughts may look like:

"I am going to be really proud of myself when I complete this detox."

"I am looking forward to the stillness and the peace of this detox."

"I can't remember the last time I took a break from technology, so this is going to be an interesting experiment."

"I am determined to reach my goals and create better habits."

"I believe in myself and my ability to perform this detox."

"I am excited to experience this journey and I am going to keep track of how it feels."

That last thought touches on something that a lot of people enjoy doing during a dopamine detox—journaling. Recording your experience is a great way to stay calm and in the present while also discovering how the detox actually feels. Being able to express yourself with honesty and sincerity will help you during those minutes when you're twiddling your thumbs, wondering what to do next. Let's take a moment to summarize everything we've talked about in this chapter.

Chapter Summary

- Scientists and neurologists agree that dopamine and our body's interaction with this neurotransmitter have a lot to do with our likelihood of survival.

- Because it doesn't have the greater context, our body sees these activities as ways of surviving, as it does other dopamine-releasing activities.

- While the brain appreciates things that are pleasurable, it doesn't always consider the things that are actually healthier for our mind, body, and spirit. The brain sees pleasure and these dopamine-releasing activities *out of context*.

- A dopamine detox can be altered to suit your needs and responsibilities and to align with your work and home life.

- The only requirement necessary to perform a dopamine detox is a well-executed plan that fits in with your schedule and does not negatively impact your other responsibilities.

- Ensure that you arrange your schedule so that you have a certain amount of uninterrupted dopamine downtime. This could be part of the fun adventure of this detox. You may decide to take a trip to the country or go camping.

- You can choose to do this as part of a solo mission or bring the family/loved ones/friends on board to strengthen morale. Just remember that communication should still be kept to a minimum.

- Resetting dopamine overstimulation is all about taking a break from daily dopamine-releasing stimuli for a planned period of time.

- Social media, coffee, alcohol and drugs, music, digital entertainment, porn—all of these stimuli will be taking a back seat during your dopamine detox.

- Choose which detox suits you best. The difference between each length of time is the effectiveness. The longer you detox, the more effective this exercise is. But you don't have to do a detox all in the same couple of days. You can choose to do a 24-hour detox on one day of the week and then perform a second one the next week.

- It is better to be realistic about your addictions and habits than vow to never change them.

- Be mindful of your brain's creative ability to talk you out of something that is better for you.

- Healthy habit-building takes time, and so does positive thinking.

- Negative thinking is on average 30 times more likely to stick in our minds than positive thinking.

- Identify some thoughts that resist the idea of doing the detox and challenge them.

- Decide what your intention is with this detox and have it at the forefront of your mind.

- You have control over your thoughts, feelings, and actions. Check in with yourself and be honest about how you're feeling while ensuring that you are not giving in to resistance.

Okay, now let's move on to the fun part. In the next chapter, we are going to take a look at all of the wonderful things you *can* do while on your dopamine detox, and after that we'll look at the partial dopamine detox. We will also be discussing some ways you can increase morale and keep pushing forward during the detox. Remember that light reading is perfectly okay while on a dopamine detox. If you are losing morale or aching to reach for the remote or your phone, pick up this book and read over some of your action steps. This book is here to support you while you perform the detox, and reviewing the reasons that you're doing this, as well as the negative impacts you know your substances are having on you, will certainly increase your ability to detox mindfully.

CHAPTER FOUR

What Can I Do on a Dopamine Detox?

In this chapter, we will go into detail about what you *can* do on a dopamine detox. It is important to note that there are different variations of this brain activity. As we have seen in the previous chapter, people may choose to do this detox for different lengths of time. Many also choose to perform a partial dopamine detox, which we will investigate in Chapter Five. In a partial dopamine detox, you wouldn't be going "cold turkey" on all dopamine-hacking habits. Instead, it's about implementing daily habits that have slow-release enjoyment that will replace instant gratification habits that we don't enjoy as much and perform in a "zombie" state. Slow-release activities are tasks that are not focused on simply giving us our next hit of dopamine. An example of a slow-release activity would be something that engages the prefrontal cortex, such as learning a new language, playing an instrument, or doing a puzzle. There are also slow-release habits, such as making your bed every morning, taking vitamins and minerals, or fitting in exercise. These habits are not so focused on getting an instant hit of dopamine but rather, are beneficial over time. You see the positive effects of these habits and activities as time goes on, making them more fulfilling and less focused on instant gratification.

Earlier articles written on the subject of dopamine detoxing were fairly limited in regards to what sort of activities should be done during the detox. I have read some journalistic accounts of people who fasted as well as removing other stimuli. Such accounts tell us that the person's hunger pangs were so overwhelming that they could hardly enjoy unplugging. People fast for religious, spiritual, or medical reasons and find it valuable, but the problem with dopamine stimulation and certain foods is not the food itself. Foods that are connected to instant gratification, repetition, and high sugar or salt content fit into the no-go dopamine detox category because they produce a similar result to that of video games or social media. Such foods have little nutritional value and often leave us wanting more. There are also countless studies that discuss the negative mental impact of overconsumption of junk food. But that does not mean that all food should be avoided! In fact, if you have been overconsuming junk food or sugary drinks and are performing this detox as part of a break from that, then contact with nutritional food and home cooking can be a great accompaniment for your detox. This brings us to your first slow-releasing task that you can perform as part of your detox.

Cooking/Preparing Food

In order to avoid high-stimulating activities such as being in a packed cafe or an overwhelming grocery store, make sure to have enough food in your home so that you can relax and prepare your meals for the day. If you are someone that doesn't spend much time in the kitchen and even *dreads* cooking, then all the better! Preparing food or even preparing something as simple as a cup of tea is a great way to stay present and be mindful. Reading instructions about a task that you are not used to performing is also a great way of engaging your prefrontal cortex. When the brain sees a task that has a slower release of satisfaction, it can often be put off. That's why we reach for the take-out menu, grab a sandwich to eat on the go, or sit down to eat at a local restaurant. In fact, an article published by Business Insider found that Americans eat out nearly six times per week, on average! While there are many wonderful things about eating out—interaction with friends, no work to prepare the food, and no clean-up—there are also some downsides. Having someone else prepare your food means you have less control over what sort of ingredients are being used. Also, the financial costs are significant. Spending just $60 a week on coffee and eating out means that in one year, you will have spent over $3,000. While that might not seem like a huge cost overall, if this habit is kept up, in five years, that would amount to $15,600. Eating out in and of itself is not the issue here—most people are willing to spend a certain amount of money on a task that makes life a little bit easier. But getting take-out and avoiding cooking is very much an instant-gratification activity, one that doesn't leave us feeling as satisfied as when we cook the meal ourselves.

The satisfaction that can be achieved by preparing your own meals, even just for a couple of days, is exactly the sort of satisfaction we are looking for throughout this dopamine detox. You are performing a task that seems difficult and that may even turn you off, but the achievement of eating the food that you cooked for yourself will leave you feeling confident and more willing to take on harder tasks in the future. You are not overwhelming your dopamine receptors, especially since the foods that you are eating are going to be healthy and nutritious, which may be different from your usual daily habits. Instead, you are teaching yourself that the slow-release tasks which at first seem impossible are actually not as big a deal as you thought. And luckily for you, there won't be any distractions to prevent you from performing the clean-up after!

Some studies talk about which foods to eat and which foods to avoid when on a dopamine detox. You already know that highly processed food and salt and sugar should be avoided, but what sort of brain food will be beneficial for you and will complement this brain activity?

Food For Thought

Here is a list of foods that are specifically beneficial to the brain and are nutritious in value:

Leafy Greens

Leafy greens such as kale, spinach, butter lettuce, cabbage, and broccoli are a great accompaniment to a dopamine detox. Eating nutritious foods that aren't about instant gratification is a great way to increase momentum during your detox. Aligning your foods and beverages with your detox is going to help you keep focus while fuelling your body with what it needs. Leafy greens have plenty of vitamins, minerals, and fiber. Vitamin K, in particular, encourages healthy fats in the brain that are linked to memory and brain function. If you have been slammed at work and are reaching for the nearest sugary snack that you can find, then munching on some kale might not sound too appealing to you. But remember, that is exactly what we want. You are building better habits and essentially proving to your brain that these sorts of habits are worth developing because they have long-term, healthy benefits. If you are performing a dopamine detox for a couple of days or implementing partial detox habits, you will be able to see the positive effects of eating high-fiber and highly nutritious foods. The great thing about these fiber-rich foods is that they keep you fuller for longer. Eating foods that are not as tempting as a juicy Big Mac, but that are far more nutritious and will also help you maintain the right mindset when it comes to dopamine and food. You aren't going to get the spike of dopamine that comes from ordering take-out that can arrive in minutes. You aren't engaging your tastebuds with the idea that a reward is just around the corner. You are fuelling your body for what it needs and being mindful about it. This will help keep you in the right state of mind and will prevent you from using food as a "hit" or an indulgence during the detox. Try crisping some kale in the oven with a drizzle of olive oil, or adding spinach to a salad with pumpkin seeds, some strawberries, and balsamic vinegar. There are a hundred different ways you can enjoy salad greens, and the nutritional value is sure to compliment your brain activity.

Boiled or Steamed Vegetables

Too often, we think that in order to eat any kind of vegetable, it has to first be doused in salt, oil, or some kind of sauce. This teaches our tastebuds that food can only be enjoyable when it has been saturated with things that give instant gratification. Food is not supposed to be something that gives us a dopamine hit. Treating food like this can lead you to feel dissatisfied with simple, everyday foods, and it can also lead to a reluctance to engage with simply-cooked meals. Keep your meals simple and honest during this detox. Choose some vegetables that you enjoy such as carrots, potatoes, parsnips, peas, or corn, and prepare them with relative simplicity. Consider what you usually season your vegetables with and for a short period of time choose not to reach for flavorings. The purpose of this activity is not to say that salt and butter are bad—rather, it is to prevent your brain from seeking that instant gratification. It is also a great way of practicing mindfulness while you engage in this dopamine detox. Prepare your vegetables mindfully, observing what it takes to prepare them for cooking, be it peeling an onion or de-seeding a pepper. When you are eating your vegetables, take into consideration their tastes and identify the flavors that are naturally already there. You are not reaching for flavoring as a way of getting a quick dopamine hit. Rather, you are fuelling yourself and being mindful about it in the process. This activity has a lot to do with maintaining a relaxed state of mind. You want to avoid little traps that will give your brain an excuse to get a hit of dopamine, even if only momentarily.

Healthy Fats

Foods that contain healthy fats are an excellent way of feeding the brain and staying fuller for longer. Foods within this category include nuts such as pumpkin seeds, almonds, cashews, and peanuts. Avocados are packed with healthy fats that promote brainpower, as are fatty fish such as salmon, tuna, and mackerel. Dark chocolate, as long as it contains at least 70% cocoa, is another high-fat food with excellent health benefits. The purpose of engaging with foods that have a mixture of high fiber, fat, and protein content is that they will leave you feeling fuller for longer. When you are engaging in a well-balanced diet that promotes nutrition as opposed to instant gratification, you are less likely to obsess over what meals you are going to have and what sort of dopamine hit you can get from them. Instead, the food is serving its purpose in fuelling you and enhancing your brain's concentration and memory levels.

Caffeine-Free Teas

Teas such as decaf green tea, chamomile tea, peppermint tea, and dandelion tea are very suitable when performing a dopamine detox. Make sure to choose teas that are low or even free from caffeine, as caffeine can cause a spike in dopamine levels. These teas can have calming effects on the mind and can allow you to have a little bit more variety in your beverages instead of sticking strictly to water. Also, consider opting for sparkling water as well as still water to accompany you on your dopamine detox. Doing so will give you that bit of variety without spiking your blood sugar or dopamine levels.

Implementing a Morning Routine

How we start our day will have such an impact on how the rest of the day goes. Have you ever slept in and awakened half an hour later than usual, feeling like a total failure? For those who work from home, what does your morning routine look like? Are you used to switching on the news or some music while drinking a cup of coffee and half-browsing through emails before realizing that half your morning has flown by? The dopamine detox is the perfect opportunity to practice a morning routine that promotes stillness, peace, and productivity. You can begin by *making your bed*. This is the first task of the day and one that might cause you to feel a little resistance. Your brain may try and get you out of this productive task in the hopes of getting that hit of caffeine. *"What's the point? I'll be sleeping in it later!"* You might be familiar with the book by ex-Navy Seal William H. McRaven, called "Make Your Bed", in which he goes through ten life lessons that taught him how to lead a productive, positive life. William speaks about how grounding that simple first step in the morning can be, and how it can boost confidence for the tasks and challenges ahead. After making your bed, you may want to get a glass of water, do some stretching on your yoga mat, perform a ten-minute meditation, and then make your breakfast slowly and mindfully. A peaceful morning really does have the ability to transform the day and set us off on the right foot. The brain responds very well to positive reinforcement. Making your bed is a great way of getting over that very first simple challenge of the day and letting yourself know that you are ready for productivity. I understand that some of you will be taking care of children, pets, or other family members while engaging in the dopamine detox. I also know that mornings with children are not always linear! Whatever your morning duties are, plan them diligently and ensure that you have enough time to do the tasks that are required of you in the same consistent and routine manner. Building better habits starts with those first few hours of the day. By sticking to the same routine, you are telling yourself that you have the capability to follow through with what you have promised. This will instill confidence and trust in yourself and will help keep momentum throughout the day.

Housework

If you have been avoiding your laundry basket for a while or if your drawers need reorganizing, then the dopamine detox is a great opportunity to do just that. Once the TV is switched off, it can be tempting to twiddle your thumbs and let your mind mull over everything that you are anxious about. Keep the mind occupied by performing a productive and slow-releasing activity such as housework. Do your walls need painting? Do you have a spare-room that is full of old clothes and miscellaneous furniture you have no use for anymore? Do yourself a long-term favor and use this additional time to declutter some things in your household. You can gather some old clothes together and donate them to charity. Perhaps you have been meaning to upholster a piece of furniture but have just never found the time to do so. Whatever it is that you haven't been able to make time for, use your additional energy and TV-free time to perform tasks that you would otherwise dread and turn up your nose at. The real benefits to these sorts of tasks are the long-term satisfaction and pride that comes from the days and even weeks of life improvement, all thanks to finally getting to work. House activities on the to-do list are usually the type of thing that lives rent-free in our mind, causing us anxiety and making us feel lazy and sluggish. During a recent dopamine detox that I performed, I tackled my spare room, which was full of mismatched furniture, about three mattresses, and every piece of clothing I have ever owned since the 90s. I didn't tackle this task all at once—I allowed myself around four days to complete the clear-out, and now I use this room as a study. I am benefiting every single day from those four days of work. The clean-up didn't give me a dopamine high or instant gratification. Rather, it was a slow and steady task that I had to keep building up momentum to complete. And I'm so glad I did.

Work Responsibilities

If you are working during your dopamine detox, then your day is likely to look a little different. You may take fewer meetings, you will probably be checking your emails a lot less, and you won't be engaging in your usual dopamine-hacking procrastination activities. While I do think there is a benefit to performing a dopamine detox away from work responsibilities, working while detoxing is a great way of practicing boundaries. Try to plan your day a little differently. Since you won't have the usual distractors in place, consider a task that you have found daunting and have been avoiding but that has clear and obvious benefits to you. Perhaps you need to get started on a sales pitch that you haven't had the drive to begin, or maybe there are some boring record-keeping tasks that you've been avoiding. Choose the most daunting task to perform first and check in with yourself while you are performing this activity. Most often, our minds will consider a task far worse or more daunting than it actually is. The fear of doing a task prevents us from getting what we need to get done. If we wait for inspiration to spark, then our work is never going to be consistent in the way that we need it to be. Don't wait until the dopamine detox is over to get going on those tasks you've been avoiding. Rather, use the distraction-free time to prove to your brain that hard work really does pay off, as you will see when these positive habits start to reap their rewards.

Goal-Setting

Remember in Chapter Two when you took the time to think about some goals that you are hoping to achieve in your life? If you performed this task correctly (don't beat yourself up if you didn't—you can always do it again), then you will have a fair amount of material to reference. You will have specified which goals you are looking to achieve in the next five years. You will also have identified which goals require daily, weekly, or ongoing tasks, as well as your feelings and hesitation toward such goals. Take a moment now to reflect on what you wrote in Chapter Two and realign yourself with the goals you want to achieve.

When goal-setting, you run the risk of letting the perfectionist mindset take over, and you could begin to fantasize about all of the wonderful habits you will start to develop as your future self. The perfectionist mindset is essentially what prevents us from trying out new goals, tasks, or aspirations because the idea of getting it wrong is frightening. *Imagining* our future selves is a whole lot easier than implementing those habits within our daily lives. Instead of simply fantasizing about all of the wonderful daily habits you're going to have in the future, *start today*. A writer will often tell you that the biggest struggle with writing a book is not the writing itself, but sitting down to actually start it. Most writers who are successful in their careers have productive, regimented schedules, much like any other job, which allow them to show up every day regardless of how many words are produced on the page.

Fear can be a powerful obstacle to getting what you want out of life. Generally, the more you care about something, and the more you want to achieve it, the scarier and more anxiety-inducing getting started feels. But I promise you, once you start to show up for yourself, that overwhelming dread starts to dissipate. Instead, you begin to trust yourself and you begin to see pragmatic and practical results. When you really start to show up for yourself, you spend far less of your time fantasizing about goals and instead move on to the actual *doing*.

Looking over the goals you wrote down during Chapter Two, consider some of the hesitations or resistant feelings that you noticed when it comes to your goals.

For each resistant thought, counteract it with a productive thought. For example, if one of your goals is to increase your income in one year, perhaps you may have written negative thoughts such as:

"I don't think my boss is willing to give me more money," "Going for that promotion fills me with dread," or, *"There are no high-paying jobs in my field."*

While you are performing your dopamine detox, take the time to prepare and execute a plan that will counteract those doubts in your mind. Remember, no one ever increased their income by counting all of the ways they couldn't do it.

Instead, use this time to challenge your doubts and start figuring out ways you can get started. Is there anything that's getting in the way of taking that first leap of faith? Are evenings that could be spent chipping away at goals spent instead in front of the TV? Do you tell yourself that you don't have enough time to get started? Keeping your goals front and center in your mind while on a dopamine detox is the best way to promote positivity and productivity. While you're unplugged, you are preparing yourself for *what is to come*. Take the downtime to write some actionable goals into your calendar. Stick some post-its up on your bathroom mirror: these can be inspirational quotes that specify your goals or they can be reminders and small tasks to check off. The downtime that is benefitting your mind leaves a lot of room for mental preparation and focus. In the moments that you are a little disengaged or bored—missing the usual stimuli we rely on—recenter yourself by visualizing your goals and imagining what it would be like to step into that life right now. Visualization is an incredible tool that helps bring the subconscious mind into focus. Once the mind believes that your goals are possible, it will start actively seeking out the actions that will make them happen. We will touch on visualization more in the next chapter.

Journaling

Journaling is a great way to stay present, practice mindfulness, and engage with yourself during this dopamine detox. As a writer, I am a big fan of journaling. I have gone through phases where I have written about my life every day for a year, leaving myself with a 365-page diary of random thoughts and a structured account of each day. There are a lot of benefits to journaling. For one, it can be incredibly grounding—returning to the same notebook at the same time each day to simply record what is going on around you. The point of keeping a journal is not to write with artistic flair or to be overly detailed about things. It is simply to practice being present in the moment, acknowledging how you feel (anxiety, discomfort, peace, boredom), and simply allowing those feelings to exist. It can also be a great way of breaking up the day, especially for those who are looking for a more strict dopamine detox that includes doing as little as possible and maintaining stillness and mindfulness throughout the day.

Meditation

There is a reason that I have dedicated an entire section to meditation in this book. Meditation is one of the greatest tools that you can use to enhance your productivity and concentration. Meditation is quite simply the only time our brains are not swarmed and overrun with thoughts. This practice is deeply ingrained in human spiritual history, and the results of meditating daily can be truly remarkable. The discomfort or hesitation that can be felt the first time you meditate is perfectly natural. If you haven't practiced it before, then it can feel like you're "failing" the first time. Although visual entertainment and screens should be avoided, there are audio meditations that can be pre-downloaded that include guides and music to help get you into the right frame of mind. You may even want to take this time to meditate outside in the stillness of nature, taking in all of the natural sounds around you and enjoying simply being present, exactly where you need to be.

A Quiet Walk

If you are used to popping in your headphones every time you leave the house, then it will feel a little funny when you aren't doing this during your detox. That discomfort is good! It gets you thinking about those daily habits that may be blocking some critical thinking space. Take the time to notice the natural sounds around you. Spend some time sitting on a bench and watching the small details of nature that we often are too distracted to notice. Go somewhere that feels peaceful and that gives you the energy to maintain your discipline. Walks are a great way of breaking up the day and engaging in some physical activity that is not related to dopamine overstimulation.

Being Still, Present, Mindful

While there may be a temptation to fill your day up with tasks, the dopamine detox is not about doing things. It is about unwinding, taking a step back, and giving your brain the space it requires to reset that overstimulation caused by poor daily habits. It is a chance to prove to yourself that you are not at their mercy. In fact, you are capable of creating boundaries and new habits. Maintain a goal of staying present and feeling gratitude for this special space that you have carved out for yourself, where you have disengaged from your usual digital and social responsibilities. It is often within these moments that the best ideas are formed.

Chapter Summary

- Fasting from food entirely is not a good idea while performing the dopamine detox; the painful deprivation is likely to distract you from the larger aim of this exercise.

- Certain brain foods should be implemented in your detox plan. Foods that leave you fuller for longer, as well as foods that aren't going to cause dopamine spikes are preferred.

- The dopamine detox is a great way to start implementing your ideal morning routine. Use the extra space and time you have to your advantage: make your bed, meditate, and practice gratitude. Starting the morning right will build confidence for the day ahead.

- Performing an odd job around the house that has been neglected is a clever way of using your spare time wisely. These sorts of slow-release activities that are about long-term goals are complementary to a dopamine detox mindset. If you are going to perform some housework, keep it light.

- If you are working during your dopamine detox, use the extra time to your advantage and start tackling some of those slow-release tasks that require special concentration.

- A dopamine detox is a perfect time to check in with yourself, your goals, your progress, and your ambitions. Visualize what your life will look like once you complete those goals. Write specific actions on your calendar, holding yourself accountable for making sure they get done.

- Check in with yourself throughout the day and write down how you are feeling, honestly and non-judgementally.

- Take advantage of the quiet stillness that comes with embracing your day. Instead of replacing the outside world with headphones, take in all the noises and movements around you.

- Mindfulness and stillness are at the forefront here. Stare at a painting in the house that has been there forever. Go people-watching in the park. Take a chair and sit in front of the window, watching the world go by.

CHAPTER FIVE

The Partial Dopamine Detox

Meet Yourself Where You Are

I once had a friend who owned an extremely successful company. My friend's company—let's call him Carl— eventually grew to become one of the many tech giants in Silicon Valley. After years and years of investing, working 16-hour days, building a team from scratch, securing funding, and maintaining this stamina for nearly a decade, his company went from a small start-up to a multi-million-dollar business. During this time— understandably—Carl put all of his time and effort into his business. But around ten years or so after starting the business, he began to suffer from severe migraines. No matter what he tried—drinking excessive amounts of water, going on San Francisco healing retreats, piercing his Daith (a section of the ear that is known to reduce migraines when pierced), acupuncture, and quitting coffee and caffeine—he was still no better than before. He went to doctors and specialists and was left frustrated and without any answers as to why he began suffering from these migraines all of a sudden. Carl was struggling so much that his work was suffering. He was losing morale and enthusiasm for the company and he felt disengaged from his friends and family. He wrote to me in an email that he found he would rather be in a dark room than outside. I knew that Carl was really struggling, and even though his job and lifestyle were full of the types of responsibilities that most people might not ever come across in their lifetimes, I knew what advice I wanted to offer Carl.

It was around this time that I discovered the dopamine detox myself. I was doing research for a story that I was writing and this led me to set out on a much longer path, because I became fascinated with the modern world's daily habits and how these habits are sucking the life out of us. Once the article was published, I sent it to Carl and asked for his opinion. When he replied, "Sounds like exactly what I need," I knew he would be open to unplugging, at least for a couple of days. What happened after that was rather remarkable. Carl decided to book himself into a quaint and non-fussy hotel, so different from the five-star establishments at which he usually stayed when he was on business trips. The hotel was two hours away from the city. He left his laptop at home—something that I hadn't seen him do in over 15 years—and instead of bringing his smartphone, he opted for an old model cell phone that was simply for calls and messages. Carl brought some light reading to his hotel, as well as some trekking shoes, a yoga mat, and his old iPod that had some relaxing jazz and classical music. He was all set for his first dopamine detox. When he came home from his two-day retreat, he could not stop raving about the peace and tranquility he found up in the mountains—the pleasure of not doing anything, even though his brain was routinely ticking away, trying to set off his panic receptors. Carl was in such a state of exhaustion that he slept for a great deal of the time, did some reading, meditated for extended periods, went hiking, lay in the grass, looked up at the clouds, made some tea—and as simple as these things sound, they were exactly the sorts of activities that Carl had completely neglected for the past 15 years. In fact, it was the first time he had been on vacation in almost *five years!*

Carl was particularly interested in meditation. He has since practiced a dopamine detox every couple of months—sometimes for 24 hours, and sometimes he implements it into his work schedule and performs a partial detox. Since he first began to carve this downtime into his schedule, Carl's migraines have virtually vanished. His doctors and specialists were equally pleased for him, but not surprised.

Stress can have an incredible impact on the body. But the reason why I wanted to highlight this story is to emphasize that *goals and aspirations can look different for everybody.* You may have already seen massive success in your life. Perhaps you're in a fulfilling relationship but are still questioning your career. Maybe you are thinking about going back to college later in life, or writing a book in your seventies. Maybe—just like Carl—all you want to do in your life is find some quiet time to zen out and not be available to anyone for a while. Maybe this kind of peace seems unattainable because your responsibilities seem too intense or your start-up is just beginning to see success and you don't want to step away from it. Perhaps you are responsible for the care of an elderly or disabled family member.

I am here to tell you that no matter who you are—a brain surgeon, a parent, a college student drowning in debt, or the president of the United States—you deserve to be able to pull away. *Everyone* deserves to be able to switch off, if only momentarily, and forget about the outside world with all of its distractions. Not only this, but having that downtime and disconnecting from exterior stimuli are *essential.* You may think that being constantly available for your family, boss, or business is necessary. But the truth is, if you are not investing in self-care then you are going to suffer from burnout and are likely to crumble.

For those of you that can't see yourself performing a strict dopamine detox, or for those who would rather dip their toes into the detox before performing a more intensive version, this partial dopamine detox is a great way to start.

Essentially, what I mean by this phrase is just a customized version of a regular dopamine detox. Too often, people will consider the responsibilities of a regular detox and simply say to themselves, "Nope, can't do it. Won't do it." But not attempting some form of breaking your habits will make it very difficult to ever get relief from that pattern of overstimulation. Just because it doesn't *seem* like you can perform a regular detox does not mean you can't participate at all!

For example, you may have a tech-centered life in which taking time off is not possible at the moment. Perhaps you'd like to implement a dopamine detox along with some relaxing writing (either fiction or nonfiction) or painting. Perhaps you are performing this detox as part of a greater passion project, one that requires stillness and quiet while you prepare yourself. Whatever your reason, here is the advice I have to offer on implementing a partial dopamine detox.

The Dos and Don'ts of a Partial Dopamine Detox

- **Do** be honest with yourself about where you are, what you're capable of doing, and how you can best benefit from this detox. For example, you may not be able to take time off from your daily responsibilities, such as minding children or working an online job. If this is the case, that's perfectly fine! There are still plenty of ways you can reduce your dopamine stimuli while engaging in some essential tasks.

- **Don't** use the partial dopamine detox as an excuse to fall into poor habits. Just because you are not committing to unplugging completely, that doesn't mean you should keep up your regular behaviors. Take Carl's idea of switching from a smartphone to a simpler cell phone so that you're available, but only for essentials. Take a half-day, if your work allows it, and dedicate those few hours to a regular dopamine detox schedule, maintaining mindfulness throughout the day and taking any opportunity you can to wind down and disconnect. And then when you're off work, you can shut out the distractions for the rest of the day.

- **Do** stick to cutting out visual entertainment such as TV and movies, porn, and junk food—in other words, anything that is non-essential. Even though coffee may feel like it's essential, the break will ultimately do you good. Use the time to get extra-hydrated and reduce the spike of dopamine released from caffeine intake. Take note of how you feel as the time goes by as you cut these things out.

- **Do** let classmates, work colleagues, or family members know that you are partaking in a partial dopamine detox. Again, the partial detox can be performed within your daily schedule, but the way you'll be living will still be different from usual. Instead of meeting friends after class, you may choose to sit in the park quietly by yourself. Instead of attending an intensive fitness class, you could stick to meditation or light stretching.

Instead of watching television at night, enjoy writing in your journal without the distraction of music or other entertainment.

- **Do** ditch social media apps. You may choose to perform the partial dopamine detox because you are unable to take time off from work. Perhaps these apps even provide you with your income stream, either business or personal. Still, the addictive nature that these things have implemented into their designs is a nightmare of overstimulation. Engaging in social media during a dopamine detox will not make for an effective break. If you do have a job that requires a lot of contact with the social media world, then perhaps a 24-hour detox will suit you better. Even the most important people in the world take time off. I promise you, the digital world is not going anywhere. In fact, if you do have an online presence, perhaps you can speak about your dopamine detox after you have completed it.

- **Don't** check your phone during the night and do ensure that it is out of reach for most of the day, after you've made the correct preparations. You may choose to opt for a separate alarm clock while you are taking a digital break.

- **Do** consider performing a partial dopamine detox for longer than 24 hours. In order to be really effective, from three to seven days is best. Resetting your dopamine overstimulation takes time. That is why I suggest performing a detox a couple of times per year. In fact, these sorts of grounding, stabilizing, and self-discipline-forming habits should be implemented as often as you can. The longer you abstain from dopamine stimuli, the longer the positive effects will last, and the more your new habits will take hold.

- **Do** engage in activities related to a regular dopamine detox. Remember, a well-executed plan will do wonders for your dopamine detox. It is not enough to simply tell the brain what it can't do. The brain needs options in order to feel like a task is possible. Refer back to the many activities discussed in the previous chapter and consider when and where you will plan these activities into your day.

- **Don't** allow the fear of failure to stop you from trying. If you ask me, a partial dopamine detox may require even more self-discipline than a regular one. As discussed in the previous chapter, moving temptations out of sight can really help. But with the partial dopamine detox, lines can become a little blurred and you may feel like it's ineffective and not worth trying. I promise you, reducing your daily habits and executing a more strict schedule will have positive effects on your habits, well-being, and productivity. Be disciplined and you'll increase your skills at this activity, just like any other.

- **Don't** lose momentum before you've even begun. Allow yourself to get into the flow of the partial dopamine detox. If bad habits slip in, if you end up checking your phone and staying on it for twenty minutes, if you have a glass of wine at lunch as part of someone's farewell gathering, simply tell yourself that you can start again tomorrow. Heck, you can start again in an hour! The partial dopamine detox gives you more flexibility and time to get into the flow of things and to reduce stimuli as you go along, with practice.

- **Do** ask others to join you. Get the kids to take a break from their video games or iPads, go for a family walk, and encourage your partner to switch off the TV for the evening in favor of some reading or a puzzle or a board game. It is certainly going to help your momentum for those in your environment to be aware of what you are doing. Even if they don't follow suit, you are sure to be a shining example and a great influence once people see the benefits of your unplugged life!

Chapter Summary

- A partial dopamine detox is about limiting overstimulation without getting rid of every stimulation.

- A partial dopamine detox should still omit digital entertainment and non-essentials.

- This style of dopamine detox is a great way to dip your toe in the water and get a feel for what a regular dopamine detox is like.

- While a regular dopamine detox may be more effective in resetting dopamine receptors, a lot depends on how long and how frequently you are practicing these positive habits. To see the best results, repeat this partial dopamine detox whenever you can.

- By including some family members, colleagues, or friends in the challenge.

- Don't beat yourself up if you mess up. But also, don't use a partial detox as an excuse for false starts and old habits to creep in. You are still on a different schedule than normal and that should always be considered.

Chapter Six

An Introduction to Meditation

The Work Shift

Since the pandemic erupted in early 2020, there has been a massive global labor shortage. In America alone, there are currently 2.2 million workers missing from the labor market. These jobs are some of the lower-income jobs that used to be filled by immigrants coming to live and work in America. Since COVID-19 travel restrictions, many people who used to take on these lower-income or high-risk jobs have been unable to do so. It is not only immigrants that are part of these 2.2 million workers, but also older workers who would have been at risk during the pandemic, as well as mothers.

I think it is fair to say that the COVID-19 pandemic influenced almost every part of the world at some stage. Whether families were suddenly all working under the same roof with schools and offices closing, or whether you were one of the industries that closed completely, many people's lives were upheaved. Parents and in particular, mothers, have had to leave the labor market, many of whom are yet to return as the world continues to tackle the effects of the past two years. One million of the 2.2 million workers missing from the labor market are high-educated adults. Interestingly, in a survey released by the US Conference Board, US CEOs say that labor shortages are the top threat to their businesses this year. Not only has the pandemic influenced a work-from-home revolution, but it has also allowed people to take a step back from their day-to-day lives and begin to question whether working in a company full-time is what they really want to do for a large sum of their day. At the start of the pandemic, companies were turned on their heads and suddenly, any industry that could function with people working at home needed to prove they could do so. The pressure of performing at even the same level as when workers have offices, unlimited wifi connections, and no disturbances from kids or animals was great. In fact, it has left many people claiming that they have suffered burnout.

This worldwide burnout is something that the World Health Organization (WHO) believes will cost billions in the labor market. WHO has estimated that labor shortages, as well as global burnout, could come into full effect within the next ten years, costing the world an annual excess of 300 billion dollars. In other words, if companies and industries alike do not respond to their workers' claims of running on empty, then this labor shortage could increase.

A Different Way of Thinking

Dr. Joe Dispenza, a neuroscientist and avid meditator, says that by the time a human being is thirty years old, the brain is running on auto-pilot as much as 95% of the time. That leaves a mere 5% of the mind that is conscious, that is actively thinking and trying to think new, better thoughts. But for the other 95% of the time, we are repeating daily, methodical patterns of thinking, being, and acting. Maybe you get up on the same side of the bed every day, you brush your teeth at the same time, make a cup of coffee, drink a glass of water, and eat a bowl of cereal. Maybe you grind your teeth when it hits 8:45 a.m. and you are stuck in traffic again, you may feel a pulse of stress and feel exasperated by the number of cars on the road. If you work in an office, perhaps you take coffee breaks at the same time each day or speak to the same people at lunch. You probably have some meetings that occur weekly or even daily, you get home, have some dinner, check your phone, and switch on the T.V, unwinding from the day that is fairly similar to the next. The problem with this auto-pilot way of living is that many of us are repeating the same patterns as the day before and feel unable to create newer, better habits. Perhaps you want to carve some time in your day to work on a passion project, but between getting to work, picking the kids up from school, and preparing the dinner, you can't seem to find the time. As statistics show, part of the reason for this global labor shortage has come from direct impacts due to the pandemic:

mothers staying home when schools and childcare facilities were closed, immigration laws changing during COVID-19, and older workers more vulnerable. But there are the other percentages of people who simply started to realize that perhaps, there was a different way of doing things. What if you didn't have to work in an office 9-5, five days per week? What if you could blend childminding with work and share the tasks between you and a partner or family member? What if you didn't have to leave your house at all to work and instead, could set yourself up with a laptop and sit in your pj's, leaving the traffic jams and awkward canteen talk behind?

Suddenly, there was a different way of doing things: a different way of working. This has also led to a different way of thinking. Many of the day-to-day hustle and bustle activities we engage in have gone under a microscopic lens during the pandemic, while almost every country in the world saw at least one month where city and town lockdowns were in place. The world was given a time of reflection and configuration, one that allowed many people to change their careers, choose to perform the same tasks at home rather than in an office, or even quit their jobs completely, taking a longer break from work than intended. After a devastating few years that saw almost every family suffer from COVID-19 in some way, whether it was through routine or through health conditions, people have gotten a newfound perspective on life and how to manage their time. In fact, this may be one of the reasons you picked up this book and decided to work on some habits that are no longer working for you.

With a different way of living comes a different way of thinking. If before, you used to grind your teeth at the same time every day during a certain bout of traffic but have now eliminated that stress from your life, this does not necessarily mean you won't get stressed during intervals in the day. In fact, working from home does not remove a person from living on auto-pilot. Dr. Joe Dispenza estimates that people all across the world are producing the stress response hormone way more frequently than what is necessary. He states that some are operating in the stress response mode around 70% of the time. The stress response hormone, known for trying to warn us against a threat of danger, can have detrimental effects on our mental and physical health.

Kevin Janks from Centered Meditation informs us that it can take the body an entire hour to return back to its original state once the stress response hormone has been triggered. (Janks, AAMI) He says that this leads us to spend an extended amount of time recovering from that stress response. The stress response can be triggered by something as simple as no coffee in the press to an email entering your inbox that you didn't anticipate to something more serious such as losing a client. Now, think about the body and its tendency to produce the stress response hormone on occasions where it is not necessary, and consider how the body and the mind would react to say, a global pandemic. Social media, online media, and the web have made it so that when a global event occurs, there are endless amounts of information to gorge on and to feed the stress response. Worried about COVID-19? You should be! Here are a billion reasons why.

Moreover, a lot of these global events often include a division of sorts between two sides. People are becoming more and more divided by their viewpoints and this is disconnecting communities from igniting during these occasions and rallying together. Global events and fast-pacing news also mean that people are hardly ever switched off from what's going on outside in the world. Our minds are busier than ever and with the constant presence of phones, apple watches, and portable electronic devices of all kinds, it means that our minds hardly ever get a break. Going into the "stress response" so consistently can have short and long-term effects on our health, such as anxiety, digestive problems, high blood pressure, cardiovascular health, poor sleep, and total burnout. This is where meditation comes in.

What Is Meditation?

The first thing to realize is that going into the stress response mode, and the brain's ability to think of the *worst-case scenario* before the *best-case scenario* is actually the brain's natural design. **Cognitive bias** is the brain's way of filtering events and our perception and understanding of things in such a way that it intends to suppress us from danger. But this *worst-case scenario* way of thinking can actually have detrimental effects on our mental health, as well as our experiences and accomplishments. In prehistoric times, it was far more important to know which plants were going to kill you, as opposed to which plants tasted delicious. That is why our brain is predisposed to thinking **negative thoughts**. But the threat of survival is not as great as it once was. One purpose of meditation is to simply surrender to the present moment and to prevent the mind from mindlessly thinking on a loop, like it usually does. With meditation, the brain, the mind, and the body are finally getting a break from being in constant fear of danger. You are simply being. The results of this mental practice are truly mind-blowing.

If you have ever gone on a shopping spree and treated yourself mindlessly spending, you might be able to relate to the aftermath of not being very happy, even though you have listened to what you thought you wanted. The whole concept of dopamine overstimulation stems from the thought that being happy equates to getting something outside of ourselves. When we recognize this, our search for meaning turns inward. This means that we start to look to ourselves to answer that which we desire, and not at external things that are not always good for us.

In today's society, there are several different practices and purposes related to meditation. As a verb, to meditate means to ponder, to think upon. This definition can leave the purpose of meditation open and fluid. For example, you may meditate on a decision you are about to make or on your feelings about or reactions to a certain situation. You may even find yourself meditating on the social issues of today's society.

But to meditate, as part of yoga and meditation, means to come to a state of consciousness and to erase the distractions from our thoughts, as a way of relaxing the body, mind, and sensory apparatus.

When we are connected in both a physical and mental sense, we are present and we recognize our senses, while also not judging the meaning of the senses and the thoughts that come into our mind. This is why, in guided meditation, you will be asked to consider the senses around you, outside noise, scents or smells, how your body feels in that moment, etc. The perfect balance of being both observant and detached is what makes meditation possible.

Of course, concentration is not the only principle of meditation. You don't need to feel intimidated when considering whether this level of balanced concentration and awareness is even possible for you. This will all come in time. Meditation is ultimately an overpowering sense and state of complete awareness.

Concentration means directing our mind onto something that appears as an object, but that is connected to us in some way. We recognize this object as something meaningful and a part of us. In order to enter the meditative state, it is necessary to connect with an object, such as a candle burning, and put all of our concentration and meaning into this object. Connecting yourself to this object in meditation is a way of identifying how everything is connected. The more you tap into this thought, the closer you are getting to what yogis refer to as enlightenment.

Let's consider the development of a relationship between you and a parent, for example. The first time you make contact with your parents is usually when you are born. This contact is physical, as you connect skin to skin with your mother once she has given birth to you. At a young and helpless age, you learn to go to your mother for nurturing, attention, and care. If you cry, she picks you up. If you are hungry, she feeds you. If you are tired, she brings you to bed. The natural connection we have with our mother and the mother's ability to play her role accordingly has a huge impact on how we develop as people.

The connection between mother and child develops and forms according to how both respond to one another and how well the child's needs are met. When a connection is important to you, you merge with this person and form a deep sense of connectivity. We also see this in marriage a lot.

In meditation, it is believed that the cause of human suffering is due to the thoughts and the perceptions we hold onto about the world. It also believes that a distance from the natural world can make us feel totally distant from everything. Meditation is a means of trying to get that connection at the forefront of your mind so that it leaves you with a sense of belonging and togetherness. It has a lot to do with self-love and self-actualization.

Brain Wave Activity

Brain wave activity, known as brain electroencephalograph (EEG), keeps a record of our mental state. When we are awake, the mind is in a constant state of thought. These thoughts shift and move, making the EEG respond in different ways, which shows brain waves that are rapid and fast-moving.

When the mind is calm and has a chance to omit thought control, the EEG shows waves that are calm and less rapid. The deeper you go into meditation, the more these waves slow down, allowing a break from that constant state of thinking, which has been recorded as well by EEG scans. Brain studies on meditation have found that the brain produces theta waves in the frontal and middle areas of the brain when one meditates. These theta waves occur when the body and brain is relaxed and cleared of intentional thinking. These waves are responsible for our inner experiences. The concentration on the inner self during meditation is likely what allows these theta waves to be produced. For experienced meditators, these waves will be more frequent. The more you meditate, the greater the brain can handle reactions to everyday experiences, since you are spending intimate time with that part of your brain in a relaxed, technical state.

Physical benefits that occur from this reaction are everything from lower blood pressure, less perspiration, and lowering of stress levels. It is clear that meditation is a beneficiary action, and not only have brain studies recorded this, but mental health and psychology studies.

Meditation has been diagnosed for those that undergo a stressful lifestyle. Reducing stress does so much for your physical health as well as your mental health. The stress hormone being activated constantly can have cardiovascular effects on the body, raise blood pressure, and increase the likelihood of anxiety and depression. Meditation reduces the activation of the stress hormone since the brain has been able to "rest" and knows that it is allowed to rest routinely (if you practice a regular schedule).

Our brain filters information and will attach it to a thought that we already know. Have you ever wondered why, when you look down, you cannot see your nose? It is right underneath your eyes, surely you should be able to see it, and it should block your vision slightly. The brain understands that it is not important for you to see your nose when looking down, so it literally filters part of it out.

Now, consider some thoughts that have been attached to negativity biases that are causing you harm. Consider how additional thoughts make the original thought even stronger. Meditation allows us to get a cleanse from our thoughts. For a couple of minutes, our brain is not working overtime to try and process a huge amount of information.

If you suffer from depression and anxiety, then your brain may be in a panic mode more often than others, which can be exhausting and difficult to manage. Meditation should leave you feeling alert, aware, and a lot more present.

Dopamine Detox and Stillness

Mindfulness will be essential for your dopamine detox. As well as practicing meditation, engage with mindfulness throughout your detox by taking in the natural sounds you hear. Consider how much of our everyday life is saturated with noise, constant sounds filling our eardrums and debilitating us from thinking clearly. When you are detoxing, reflect on how many new sounds you are hearing and actually paying attention to for the first time. It can be very peaceful, taking in the natural sounds that are there and that occur, unnoticed. This is a great way of remaining in the present moment and taking in your surroundings. Whether it's the hum of the oven, birds chirping and singing their songs of praise, the plop of your goldfish splashing about in its bowl, the churn of the elevator in your building, children playing outside, waves gently crashing: all of these natural sounds suddenly become a lot more magical when they are all you have.

Check in with what sorts of sounds you hear throughout the day. Instead of rejecting them or feeling angry at them, in the same way that you would accept them during meditation, accept them into your current reality.

In fact, you can engage with all five of the senses during your dopamine detox. Since there will be so many distractions missing from your schedule, you can take the time to consider how you feel about the crunch in your cereal, the zest of lemon from the wedge in your glass of water, the squelch of your trainers after rain has fallen on a muddy day. The senses are a great way of staying present in the current moment you are in. It helps to bind you to the present surroundings and can be especially impactful for people who are feeling anxious or out of their bodies. Senses help to allow us to make sense of the world and understand what is going on around us. One thing you can do while being on the dopamine detox is start every day by planting your bare feet on a patch of green grass or earth. Connecting your feet to the earth is a great way of "grounding" oneself and appreciating being.

Conclusion

Meditation's sharp awareness with both the body and mind can see a reduction in a person's chronic stress patterns, says Dr. Nevins of The American Osteopathic Association. Meditation enables the mind to become aware and to reach a state of calmness and tranquility. It encourages and strengthens concentration. This level of self-awareness can further allow a person to detect issues with their body, says Dr. Nevins, "this concentration and sharpened self-awareness is particularly beneficial because it can help with early detection of physical problems and allow for early preventive action." (Dr. Nevins, 2021)

The practice of concentration, self-awareness, and tranquility, as well as the physically recorded reduction in EEG brain waves are all ways that yoga promotes positive wellness when practiced regularly. Also, the mantra in yoga of unity, the ability to meet socially with like-minded people, and the continual search for happiness inward all point to improved mental health and positive wellbeing.

Let's take a moment to summarize all that we have learned in this chapter:

Chapter Summary

- Since the pandemic erupted in early 2020, there has been a massive global labor shortage.

- Many people find it difficult to separate work life and home life, in particular since the global pandemic.

- The problem with this auto-pilot way of living is that many of us are repeating the same patterns as the day before and feel unable to create newer, better habits.

- **Negativity bias** is the brain's way of filtering events and our perception of things in such a way that is supposed to prevent us from danger but can actually be the cause of a lot of mental grief and suffering.

- In early survival, it was far more important to know which plants were going to kill you, as opposed to which plants tasted delicious. That is why our brain is predisposed to thinking **negative thoughts**.

- An unmanaged mind is one where thoughts are not questioned. This means that the mind dictates the emotions of a person, who then may feel like they cannot "control" their emotions when in fact, they are not controlling their thoughts surrounding those emotions.

- Going into the "stress response" so consistently can have short and long-term effects on our health, such as anxiety, digestive problems, high blood pressure, cardiovascular health, poor sleep, and total burnout.

- Meditation is a way of surrendering to the present moment and acknowledging that this moment of peace and serenity is valuable and worthy of your attention.

- Meditation is a methodology that comes from the yogic tradition.

CHAPTER SEVEN

Post-Detox Daily Habits

"Amateurs wait for inspiration to strike while the pros get up and get to work."
—Harvey Mackay

Before I learned how my daily habits were negatively impacting my life, I had countless excuses why I was not getting enough done. I would spend hours sitting and staring at my computer screen, not doing any work and at a total standstill. This was something that happened most weeks. I used to give away at least two days a week to "not feeling it," or days where the creativity just wasn't there. But this way of thinking is another way that the human brain tries to convince us not to do that thing that we are really excited about.

Resistant thoughts would pop into my head, convincing me that I was in a particular funk that day and wouldn't be able to perform as normal.

"I'm not feeling inspired."

"I'll get more done once I take a nap or watch a show on Netflix or scroll through my phone some more."

"This work is too hard—I need a break (even though I haven't done anything yet.)"

"Tomorrow will be better."

Do these thoughts sound familiar? It was clear that I was seeking activities that didn't take any effort. As soon as I made the decision to switch to something completely unrelated to my work, I was essentially giving up.

Regardless of whether you need to prepare for an exam, write a business proposal that could bring you your next big client, fix up your qualifications, or do something you're passionate about, the only real way of getting there is by putting in the work. In order to change our current reality, *we must start investing in our desired reality.* The truth is, no one cares about your goals or aspirations as much as you do! The only person who is going to be able to achieve those goals is you.

Stephen Pressfield talks at length about the deadly disease he calls resistance. In his book, *The War of Art*, Pressfield goes into detail about how resistance can ultimately bury us. He believes that the more you want something, the more resistance you are going to feel about it. That is because it is so important to you. The fear of not doing it can be confused with the fear of getting started. Resistance is a normal part of life. It is quite simply the brain's way of getting out of doing things. Resistance's best friend is known as procrastination. Procrastination is a dangerous tool that tells us the lie that we are not quitting work for the day; we are simply putting it off for a little while. Remember when I briefly mentioned the perfectionist mindset and how it has the ability to draw us into fantasizing about a reality that might never happen? Well, resistance *ensures* that it doesn't happen.

As I mentioned before, the brain can get really creative when thinking of reasons for you not to do something that is ultimately good for you, especially if you have been struggling with daily habits that are messing with your dopamine receptors. Low-value rewards are only more attractive because the brain doesn't understand which rewards are worthwhile and which rewards are bad habits. It is up to you, the master of your own mind, to learn the difference and act accordingly.

At this point, if you have already completed a dopamine detox, then you may already be performing more life-sustaining habits. But it is very easy to slip into old brain patterns. As I keep repeating, *neurons that fire together wire together.*

The truth is, *actions* are what will get you to where you need to be. Fighting resistance will also become very important for you.

If you are afraid of slipping back into old habits as soon as your dopamine detox is done, here is some advice that will ensure you stay on the right track.

Sleep, Exercise, Diet, Repeat

Sleep: Are you someone who feels chronically tired? Have you noticed that people often talk about low energy and an unexplained feeling of exhaustion? Well, if you have come this far in the book, then you already know that a lot of that fatigue comes from engaging in activities that are draining your energy.

Scrolling through your phone in a zombie-like state is certainly not going to energize you. Although this is a habit that many of us practice in our daily lives, perhaps we are less aware about the energy it takes to scroll through a seemingly endless amount of online content. When it comes to getting more energy, the tried and tested methods are always the best.

In order to give yourself the best chance at success, master your habits of sleep, exercise, and diet. Please don't oversimplify this statement. Really mastering your circadian rhythm takes a lot of time, practice, and consistency. To master positive sleep habits, consider the amount of caffeine you usually drink in a day and choose a cut-off point. Five to seven hours after you've had a cup of coffee, 50% of that caffeine is still in your bloodstream! If you have a cup of coffee at 2 p.m., then by 9 p.m., you're still trying to get rid of that last 50%. This can undoubtedly lead to interrupted sleep. Sleep is essential for goal-building and living a productive life. A good night's sleep helps balance our blood sugar levels and hormones, improves memory, forms connections, new ideas, and heals muscles in the body.

Also, consider going to bed around half an hour before you intend to fall asleep. This will give you enough time to settle down and bring your mind to a place of stillness. Try to go to bed at the same time every night. This will improve your circadian rhythm and will give you a chance to take advantage of your body's clock. If you need to, make your room darker so that you can sleep through bright early mornings.

Exercise: The wonderful thing about exercising is that the more you do it, the more energy you have. Working out is going to leave you in a better mood, with more energy than before, and has numerous other physical and psychological benefits. If you have the sort of job that entails sitting at a desk for hours at a time, consider going for a jog or a walk first thing in the morning. Moving your body and getting your blood pumping first thing gets rid of all that stale blood from sleeping the night before. Moving your body first thing in the morning will pump your organs with the necessary fresh blood and oxygen. It will have a great impact on your mood and energy for the rest of the day. Really committing to this is central in maintaining your goals.

Diet: The thing about practicing good sleep and exercise habits is that this actually allows for more flexibility when it comes to diet. I am a firm believer that food should be enjoyed and that restrictions should not control a person's life. We have identified the types of foods that can be addictive and can cause problems with dopamine overstimulation. But as the old saying goes, balance really is key.

Dopamine Detox Daily Habits

What were some habits that you enjoyed during your dopamine detox, and what were the reasons you enjoyed them? Whether it was working on a complicated puzzle, washing the dishes, or committing to a morning routine, consider implementing some of these dopamine detox habits into your everyday life. For example, you may want to set boundaries on how much you use your phone in the evening. You might decide you've had enough of that video game that's taking away all of your attention and ditch it for good. You may enjoy taking quiet walks instead of walks accompanied by music if only to practice the mental habit. Don't be afraid to keep the practices of your dopamine detox in your present reality, especially when you are aiming for the best version of yourself.

Recognize Resistance and Do it Anyway

The best thing you can do for yourself is to identify when you are feeling resistance about a certain task and to *do it anyway*. Understand that resistance is a part of life—it is the brain's reaction to doing anything that requires work. The brain would rather have an easy life where it can repeat the same neurons to fire and wire together forever, but that is not what truly fulfills the human mind. For this very reason, we were designed with a mind that has the ability to make better choices.

Be the master of your own fate and get to work. Ignore the distractions that are designed to empty our pockets and bring us down. As Samuel Thomas Davies says, self-discipline is about "living a life by design, not by default. But most importantly, it's acting in accordance with your thoughts—not your feelings."

Create Uninterrupted Work Blocks

One of the best ways I can ensure that I get uninterrupted writing time is by setting aside specific time to do just that. Neuroscientists estimate that the brain can concentrate very well on one given task for 90 minutes at a time. Create 90 minute blocks where you are only working on one specific task. During these uninterrupted work blocks, close your emails, turn your phone on airplane mode, and write "DO NOT DISTURB" across your forehead if you have to. Commit to this type of uninterrupted working block at least five days per week. Repeating these sorts of habits are what will set you off from the rest and improve your concentration levels.

Create a Positive Productive Loop

The real thing that sets writers apart is their ability to create a schedule for themselves. A writer knows that waiting for inspiration to strike is simply not enough. There are going to be times in your journey toward your goals where it will be crucial and beneficial for you to find inspiration. Perhaps you want to become a chef and need to travel to expand your palate, but the real chef knows that the ultimate skill they need to work on is cooking and preparing food.

Instead of waiting for inspiration to strike at random, return to your goal often and frequently. That way, the action itself will inspire creativity and motivation. Work towards a productive loop that combines action, inspiration, and motivation together.

Don't Let Negativity Bias Stop You

Don't let your fear of doing something get in the way of actually doing it. There are two types of people in the world: the spectators—who are often full of judgment and criticisms—and the creators—who don't waste their time worrying about what others think. Instead, they work through those negative emotions and fears to get the work done anyway. The only way you can escape from criticism is by doing nothing at all, fading into the background to never be remembered. Learn how to detach your emotion from your actions, show up for yourself, and simply get started—whether your goal is meeting the right partner, making a new friend, tiling a roof, or getting an interview for a new job. It doesn't matter how insignificant or strange it may seem to someone else. You are not here to impress others. There is no greater feeling than doing something for yourself only because it brings you genuine satisfaction and life-affirming happiness.

Chapter Summary

- Mastering sleep, diet, and exercise takes more time than you think. Focus on getting your body into the best rhythm you can and see the fruits of your labor.

- Caffeine intake is often an overlooked reason that

people struggle with sleep.

- Implementing some dopamine detox habits into your daily life can have a powerful impact on your overall productivity.

- Recognizing resistance for what it is—a block toward getting what you want out of life—is essential. Feel the fear and do it anyway.

- Create work blocks that benefit your schedule and that give you uninterrupted working space.

- Action, inspiration, and motivation go hand-in-hand. But action is the driving force of the three. The more you chip away at something, the more it develops and builds.

- Negativity bias is just another way our brain tries to protect us from danger. Only a lot of the time, it takes things out of context. Don't let your actions be ruled by your emotions. It is ok to feel afraid. Anything worth having will feel scary at first. That just means you care about it deeply.

Final Words

Now that we have arrived at the end of the book, it is time to implement all that you have learned and put it into action. You are in the best position to start instilling positive, more productive habits that will give you slow-release, long-term benefits. By this stage, you understand that a lot of our modern activities are stealing our dopamine and leading us into a state of overstimulation, where nothing feels enjoyable anymore. But you are one step ahead of everyone else. Now, you understand that you have the ability to practice and implement boundaries and restrictions that can change your life. Instead of being ruled by your daily habits, you are ready to master them! You are clearer than ever before about the goals you want to achieve and you have even taken specific time to schedule action steps, to visualize what you want out of life, and to start creating distance from the things that take you further away from your goals.

I want you to know that even if you have not yet performed the dopamine detox, I am proud of you. I believe that you have the utmost potential to get everything that you want out of your life. And by reading and engaging with this book, you have proven just that. Remember to come back to this book when you are feeling like you are in the same place as before. A dopamine detox can be performed as often as you like. It should certainly not be considered a crazy thing to unplug for a short period of time, and if you have already begun to implement these habits into your life, then you already know this!

Gaining distance from the things that negatively control our lives is always a good idea. Regardless of what type of dopamine detox you choose to practice and for how long, you are creating that essential bookmark in your life. You are proving to yourself that you are capable and willing to build better habits. I hope that the advice and teachings in this book have a positive impact on your life and that you recognize your massive potential. If you have enjoyed this book, please consider leaving a review so that others can also benefit from the things you've learned.

I wish you well in your journey, and I hope I get to hear about all of the wonderful things you have started filling your life with now that you are free from dopamine overstimulation and in control of your own story.

Thank You

Before you leave, I'd just like to say, thank you so much for purchasing my book.

I spent many days and nights working on this book so I could finally put this in your hands.

So, before you leave, I'd like to ask you a small favor.

Would you please consider posting a review on the platform? Your reviews are one of the best ways to support indie authors like me, and every review counts.

Your feedback will allow me to continue writing books just like this one, so let me know if you enjoyed it and why. I read every review and I would love to hear from you. To leave a review simply scan the QR code below or go to Amazon.com, go to "Your Orders" and then find it under "Digital Orders".

Scan a QR Code Below to Leave a Review:

Amazon US

Amazon Uk

References Cited

Mara Carrico (2007) *A Beginner's Guide to Meditation,* Outside Yoga Journal, https://www.yogajournal.com/meditation/how-to-meditate/let-s-meditate/

The Slow Home Podcast (2021) *How To Meditate With Kevin Janks,* Slow Your Home, https://www.slowyourhome.com/blog/149

American Osteopathic Association, (2022) *The Benefits of Yoga,* https://osteopathic.org/what-is-osteopathic-medicine/benefits-of-yoga/

Stephen Pressfield, (2002) *The War of Art: Break Through the Blocks and Win Your Inner Creative Battles*

Linda Hill

Made in the USA
Middletown, DE
26 October 2023